CANADIAN CITIZENSHIP MADE SIMPLE

A PRACTICAL GUIDE TO IMMIGRATION AND CITIZENSHIP IN CANADA

CANADIAN CITIZENSHIP MADE SIMPLE

A PRACTICAL GUIDE TO IMMIGRATION AND CITIZENSHIP IN CANADA

Joe Serge

DOUBLEDAY CANADA LIMITED

CANADIAN CATALOGUING IN PUBLICATION DATA
Serge, Joe.
    Canadian citizenship made simple

ISBN 0-385-25383-4

1. Citizenship – Canada. 2. Canada – Emigration and
immigration. I. Title.

JL187.S47 1993   323.6'0971   C92-095633-5

Cover and text design by Tania Craan
Cover illustration by John Etheridge

Printed on ∞ acid-free paper
Printed and bound in Canada

Published in Canada by
Doubleday Canada Limited
105 Bond Street
Toronto, Ontario
M5B 1Y3

To Canadians by birth and those by choice,
to the pioneers and immigrants
— nation builders all.

Contents

PART THREE

Questions and Answers 141

CONCLUSION 165

LIST OF TABLES

APPENDICES

GLOSSARY 205

ACKNOWLEDGEMENTS

I wish to thank *The Toronto Star* for the opportunity to write about immigration and citizenship matters for more than 20 years.

Any materials previously published by *The Toronto Star*, the Department of Employment and Immigration, and the Department of Multiculturalism and Citizenship are reprinted in this book with their kind permission.

Special thanks to Milton Best of Immigration Canada (Ontario Region) for his patience and kind assistance in gathering and reviewing material for the Immigration section of this book. I also thank Len Westerberg and the Federal Department of Multiculturalism and Citizenship for their assistance in compiling material for the Citizenship section. In addition, I wish to thank Susan Folkins, my editor at Doubleday, as well as Freda Hawkins and Cheryl Dudgeon, who both reviewed the manuscript, for all of their valuable and helpful suggestions.

INTRODUCTION

Every year, for the remainder of this decade, about 250,000 people will be admitted to Canada as immigrants. This annual flow of newcomers into the country is a highly significant part of Canada's population growth. Indeed, a freeze on immigration would soon cause a sharp decline in Canada's population, which has risen from approximately 5 million at the beginning of this century to more than 27 million.

Since Confederation in 1867, more than 13 million immigrants have come to Canada (see Table 1). The largest waves of immigrants came shortly before World War I broke out. In 1911, a total of 331,288 immigrants settled in Canada, in 1912, 375,756. And in 1913, 400,870 took up residence in this country — the largest influx of immigrants in any one year. In the entire 1910–19 period, the total number of immigrants to Canada amounted to 1,860,269.

The numbers were also impressive in the following decade. From 1920 through 1929 and the Depression,

Table I
IMMIGRATION TO CANADA SINCE CONFEDERATION

Year	Number of Immigrants						
1867	10,666	1899	44,543	1931	27,530	1963	93,151
1868	12,765	1900	41,681	1932	20,591	1964	112,606
1869	18,630	1901	55,747	1933	14,382	1965	146,758
1870	24,706	1902	89,102	1934	12,476	1966	194,743
1871	27,773	1903	138,660	1935	11,277	1967	222,876
1872	36,758	1904	131,252	1936	11,643	1968	183,794
1873	50,050	1905	141,465	1937	15,101	1969	161,531
1874	39,373	1906	211,653	1938	17,244	1970	147,713
1875	27,382	1907	272,409	1939	16,994	1971	121,900
1876	25,633	1908	143,326	1940	11,324	1972	122,006
1877	27,082	1909	173,694	1941	9,329	1973	184,200
1878	29,807	1910	286,839	1942	7,576	1974	218,465
1879	40,492	1911	331,288	1943	8,504	1975	187,881
1880	38,505	1912	375,756	1944	12,801	1976	149,429
1881	47,991	1913	400,870	1945	22,722	1977	114,914
1882	112,458	1914	150,484	1946	71,719	1978	86,313
1883	133,624	1915	36,665	1947	64,127	1979	112,096
1884	103,824	1916	55,914	1948	125,414	1980	143,117
1885	79,169	1917	72,910	1949	95,217	1981	128,618
1886	69,152	1918	41,845	1950	73,912	1982	121,147
1887	84,526	1919	107,698	1951	194,391	1983	89,157
1888	88,766	1920	138,824	1952	164,498	1984	88,239
1889	91,600	1921	91,728	1953	168,868	1985	84,302
1890	75,067	1922	64,224	1954	154,227	1986	99,219
1891	82,165	1923	133,729	1955	109,946	1987	152,098
1892	30,966	1924	124,164	1956	164,857	1988	161,929
1893	29,633	1925	84,907	1957	282,164	1989	192,001
1894	20,892	1926	135,982	1958	124,851	1990	214,430
1895	18,790	1927	158,886	1959	106,928	1991	226,596
1896	16,835	1928	166,783	1960	104,111		
1897	21,716	1929	164,993	1961	71,689		
1898	31,900	1930	104,806	1962	74,586		

Reprinted by permission of Employment and Immigration Canada.

1,264,220 immigrants settled in Canada. In the post-war years, large numbers of displaced persons and other immigrants from war-torn Europe came to Canada to seek jobs and a new lease on life for themselves and their families. More than 400,000 immigrants moved to Canada between 1945 and 1949, and more than 1.5 million arrived in the 1950s. Altogether, about 6,300,000 immigrants have made Canada their home since the end of World War II.

In the early years, up until the 1960s, immigration policy favoured whites, primarily those of British or European origin. More recent legislation has created a universal immigration policy that gives people of all nationalities and races an equal opportunity to immigrate to Canada — subject to conditions established by the point-system regulations.

The new policy has triggered waves of non-traditional immigrants, from places including Hong Kong, the Indian sub-continent, the Caribbean, the Middle East and Vietnam.

In the past three years, more than 82,000 people have come from Hong Kong to settle in Canada. Many are business people or professionals. In 1992, the top ten immigrant source countries, as of September 30, were Hong Kong (31,309); Sri Lanka (9,424); India (9,344); the Philippines (8,718); Poland (8,600); China (7,080); Taiwan (6,038); Britain (5,474); the U.S.A. (5,317); and Iran (5,133). More than 91,000 Vietnamese people have immigrated to Canada in the past decade. (See Appendix 1 for a list of the countries of origin of the top ten immigrant groups each year since 1968.)

As these numbers suggest, immigration has a strong impact on regional and provincial population strategies. The Canadian Immigration Act, therefore, provides a legal basis for the federal government to consult the provinces regarding the distribution and settlement of newcomers to this country. The act encourages federal–provincial agreements on immigration policy and programs. Quebec, for example, has signed the most comprehensive agreement with the federal government involving matters related to immigration, demography and employment.

The agreement between the federal government and Quebec states that the landing of immigrants in Quebec requires Quebec's prior consent. The agreement allows those approved by Quebec to qualify for immigrant visas even when they obtain only as few as 30 points in the federal points system criteria, which normally demands a score of at least 70 points to qualify. It also allows Quebec to decide who meets the standards for sponsoring relatives, and makes similar conditions for the processing of contract workers and others seeking temporary admission. Quebec immigration officials operate from Canadian consulates and Quebec missions overseas.

The Quebec government's strong involvement in immigration reflects its goal to protect French culture in that province. However, other than this emphasis on French language and cultural connections, Quebec's laws remain close to federal objectives and the federal government has the final say on who may be admitted to Quebec or any other part of Canada. This book does not delve into provincial–federal agreements. Those wishing to know more about Quebec's policies should contact authorities in that province.

After consultation with the provinces and various organizations and institutions, the federal government sets an annual immigration level. However, such quotas or targets may be increased or curbed to reflect unforeseen social or economic circumstances.

Most of Canada's immigrants enter the country as sponsored family class relatives and dependents. Others gain admission as independent immigrants or as entrepreneurs and investors, who are given special consideration because they bring business skills and money to Canada.

Of the 250,000 immigrants targeted for "landing" (permission to live in Canada) in 1993, approximately 58,000 will be refugees. About 13,000 refugees are annually airlifted to Canada under a federal government program. Approximately 20,000 are sponsored by private groups and organizations, and another 25,000 are processed for landing from within Canada. Others claim refugee status from within Canada after arriving under the guise of visitors.

In one way or another all those who seek admission to Canada are governed by Canada's complex immigration and citizenship laws. *Canadian Citizenship Made Simple* explains how to make your way through the maze of government services and regulations; it gives you straight answers to your queries concerning immigration and citizenship in Canada. Additional information and explanations that you may find helpful can be found in the various tables scattered throughout the text, and in the appendices and the glossary of terms at the back of the book. There is also a special Question and Answer section, which covers a wide range of topics and countries, and deals with some of the most frequently-asked questions concerning immigration and citizenship.

PART ONE

Immigration

CHAPTER ONE

The History of Immigration

From the early days of immigration, the flow of new-comers was pegged to Canada's need for workers — especially farm labourers. Early immigration legislation emerged from Section 95 of the British North America Act, which linked immigration with agriculture and gave each of the provinces considerable sway over both.

The first Canadian legislative measure affecting immigration dates to pre-Confederation times. An Act Respecting Aliens was passed in the first Parliament of Lower Canada in 1794. In part, it provided for the screening of immigrants on political grounds. It was primarily aimed at Americans, who were widely considered to be opposed to the British crown. Under this act, commissioners were empowered to deny admission to those considered "unlikely to become loyal and suitable settlers."

A similar act, entitled The Aliens of Nova Scotia, was passed in 1798. Nova Scotia passed several laws governing immigrants, including an act in 1828, which stated that a ship's passengers couldn't disembark until the master of the vessel had posted bonds to guarantee that they wouldn't fall on public welfare in their first year in Canada, "by reason of disease, bodily infirmity, age, childhood or indigence."

Not much later, Nova Scotia, New Brunswick and Lower Canada all imposed a head tax on every immigrant. The money was targeted for the care of sick and destitute immigrants and to help newcomers continue their journey across the land to their final destinations.

After Confederation, from July 1867 to March 1892, immigration became the responsibility of the federal Department of Agriculture. An act in 1869 brought tough restrictions governing immigrants and visitors on the basis of health and financial means. It barred admission to paupers and destitute immigrants, and provided for medical examinations of new arrivals and the detention of ailing newcomers in quarantine stations. It also required the posting of a $300 bond "for every lunatic, idiot, deaf, dumb, blind or infirm person" not belonging to an immigrant family, if that person was considered likely to become a public charge.

Immigration came under the domain of the federal Department of the Interior in 1892. In 1906 the Immigration Act was extended to provide tougher controls and immigration authorities began to hold inquiries at ports of entry. The new law also introduced measures to deport immigrants who, within two years of arrival, had become public charges or were imprisoned, or admitted to a hospital or a home for the poor, or had committed a crime involving moral turpitude.

The first act restricting and regulating Chinese immigration into Canada was given assent on July 20, 1885. It required every person of Chinese origin to pay a tax of $50 upon entering Canada. The act also provided for certain other regulations and restrictions governing the immigration of Chinese people and for the registration of Chinese residents of Canada.

On June 23, 1887, a provision was made for the exemption of women of Chinese origin who were married to non-Chinese men and wanted to embrace the nationality of their husbands. On July 18, 1900, however, the head tax was boosted to $100.

Following October 1917, immigration became the responsibility of the newly-created Department of Immigration and Colonization. On January 31, 1923, the Immigration Act restricted the admission of Chinese immigrants to female domestic servants and farm workers. The farm workers could bring with them only their wives and their children under the age of 18. Another law restricted admission of other visible minorities, unless they were United States citizens or British subjects, by reason of birth or naturalization, in Great Britain, Ireland, Newfoundland, New Zealand, Australia or the Union of South Africa. A revised Chinese Immigration Act in 1923 further toughened controls and demanded the re-registration, within 12 months of the act coming into force, of all persons of Chinese origin. The head tax was tripled to $300. As the Depression grew worse, immigration regulations became more and more restrictive and racist. Chinese people wishing to visit their country of birth were required to register on leaving, and again on returning to Canada. It wasn't until 1947 that discriminatory laws affecting people of Chinese descent were finally revoked.

The Department of Immigration and Colonization was abolished in 1936 and immigration became instead a branch of the newly-established Department of Mines and Resources. After World War II, discriminatory restrictions were gradually removed as Canadians became increasingly aware that in order to grow and prosper, Canada needed more immigrants.

On January 18, 1950, immigration operations became the jurisdiction of the newly-established Department of Citizenship and Immigration. At this time, the admissible classes were extended to include "any immigrant who satisfied the Minister that he is a suitable immigrant having regard to the climatic, social, educational, industrial, labour or other conditions or requirements of Canada; and that he is not undesirable owing to the probable inability to become readily adapted and integrated into the life of a Canadian community and to assume the duties of Canadian citizenship within a reasonable time after his entry."

In 1951, special agreements were signed to allow the annual immigration to Canada of 150 nationals of India, 100 nationals of Pakistan and 50 nationals of Ceylon. However, it is only since 1962 — with a final restriction relating to the sponsoring of relatives removed in 1967 — that Canada has offered people of all nationalities and races an equal opportunity to live here. In 1967, the National Employment Service merged with Immigration to become the Department of Manpower and Immigration, and in 1976, the Unemployment Insurance Commission merged with Manpower and Immigration to create the present Employment and Immigration Commission.

CHAPTER TWO

Canada's Immigration System

THE PRESENT LAW

Canada's immigration law is designed to be non-discriminatory and humanitarian, while encouraging Canada's social, cultural and economic development.

Because far more people wish to settle in Canada than the country can absorb, applications are considered under a broad processing system that gives priority to family reunification and refugees.

Immigration regulations are also meant to be a reflection of Canada's population and labour needs. As a condition to accepting immigrants as "permanent residents" (legal residents but not citizens), the newly amended Immigration Act empowers immigration authorities to require some immigrants to settle for up to three years in less populated parts of Canada, where their skills may be most urgently needed. This "mobility" provision is designed to allow all provinces to take advantage of the needed skills immigrants bring to Canada. It means that a skilled prospective immigrant's chances of making it to Canada may hinge on picking another part of Canada for a final destination other than the one originally intended. Applicants who voluntarily sign such contract-like agreements concerning destinations will be given special consideration by visa officers. However, for good reason, including serious illness, business failure, or other social and economic factors, such contract terms and conditions may be altered or removed. The contract requirement does not apply to sponsored family class relatives.

In addition to the regular immigration process, Canada often develops special programs for people who do not fit standard immigration categories; people such as those who are at risk, but who do not qualify as refugees according to the Geneva Convention definition. A foreign government's policies may also change to allow its nationals to emigrate. In such cases, public policy programs may be adopted in Canada to allow such people to be admitted when they would not otherwise qualify.

Amendments to the 15-year-old Immigration Act, which took effect in 1993, are intended to better control and select who comes to Canada so that immigration continues to contribute to Canada's social development and economic prosperity; by tightening up enforcement and control measures, they will protect Canadians from those who abuse Canada's immigration laws, and

streamline the refugee determination system so that
claims for refugee status from within Canada may be
more speedily heard by the Refugee Board.

THE STREAM SYSTEM

The new legislation has established a selection process
geared to three "streams". Only those who qualify
under Stream 1 are exempt from fixed annual limits.
Those in Streams 2 and 3 are subject to fluctuating
annual quotas. (See Table 2 for a projected summary of
immigration targets: 1993–95.)

Table 2
IMMIGRATION TARGETS: 1993-95

Category of Immigrant		Year	
	1993	1994	1995
FAMILY CLASS	100,000	85,000	85,000
REFUGEES: Government sponsored	10,000	13,000	13,000
Privately sponsored	9,000	15,000	15,000
REFUGEE CLAIMANTS (inland)	25,000	25,000	25,000
INDEPENDENT IMMIGRANTS: Principal applicants	35,500	40,500	40,500
Spouses and dependents	40,000	52,000	52,000
BUSINESS IMMIGRANTS: Principal applicants	7,500	5,000	5,000
Spouses and dependents	22,500	14,500	14,500

Reprinted by permission of Employment and Immigration Canada.

Stream 1 applies to family members (spouses, fiancé(e)s, and dependent children, including adopted children); those deemed to be Convention Refugees; and business persons qualifying under the Immigrant Investor Program.

Stream 2 includes parents and grandparents of Canadian residents; government-assisted and privately-sponsored refugees; those having arranged employment; the self-employed or those who apply to come to Canada as live-in caregivers; and those allowed into Canada under special programs that may be set up for public policy reasons.

Stream 3 applies to independent immigrants: those qualified in certain designated occupations; and entrepreneurs whose business experience will help boost Canada's economic development.

CATEGORIES OF IMMIGRANT

Closely related to the stream system are the three categories of immigrant:

1. Family Class
2. Refugees
3. Independent Immigrants

The "family class" is restricted to close family members, but generally excludes brothers and sisters.

"Refugees" may be airlifted to Canada under federal or private sponsorships, or be granted refugee status after being admitted to Canada as visitors or under another status.

"Independent immigrants" are selected under a point-system of immigrant selection based primarily on occupational skills and other assets that would benefit the Canadian economy. The independent immigrant's success in obtaining a visa largely rests with the visa officer's assessment of the applicant's ability to become successfully established in Canada. This category also applies to "business immigrants" — entrepreneurs, investors and those self-employed.

To obtain an immigrant visa, you must apply at a visa office operated at a Canadian embassy, consulate or high commission. In some cases, other governments, primarily U.S. and British missions in remote parts of the world, may provide immigration services. (See Appendix 3 for an address list of Canadian embassies that act as immigrant visa processing posts.)

THE POINT SYSTEM

Canada's "point system" of immigrant selection is designed to link the arrival of immigrants with Canada's labour needs. Emphasis is placed on practical training, experience and the likelihood of successful establishment in Canada.

Independent immigrants must obtain 70 points in selection criteria based on education and training, age, knowledge of English or French, demand in Canada for their work skills and other factors.

Some independent immigrants are assessed only on some of the criteria because of their specific skills or recognized abilities. Entrepreneurs and investors, for example, are not assessed on occupational demand or arranged employment factors. And, obviously, the arranged employment factor does not apply to self-employed applicants.

The point system is designed to enable the visa officer abroad to determine whether the applicant's skills are needed in Canada. In addition, the visa officer assesses the applicant's suitability as an immigrant. Thus, an application may be rejected by one visa officer and, six months later, a fresh application may be approved by another officer.

The point system does not apply to refugees and family class immigrants. In both these cases, visa officers can little affect the process because such applicants need only satisfy basic standards of good health and character. However, sponsoring relatives are required to sign an "undertaking of support" for a period of one to ten years, whatever Immigration deems necessary, as a guarantee that sponsored relatives will not become a burden on Canadian taxpayers. This is not required when sponsoring a spouse.

A waiver of the sponsor's financial obligation may later be obtained under certain conditions, including a severe loss of income and other such unforeseen economic difficulties. When a sponsor is unable to honour the sponsorship guarantee, the needy sponsored immigrant may apply for social assistance without fear of jeopardizing his or her permanent resident status.

Allocation of Points (See Table 3.)

1. **EDUCATION:** Maximum 12 points: 1 point for each successfully completed year of formal education.

2. **SPECIFIC VOCATIONAL PREPARATION:** Based on period of training or study in a specific eligible field. Maximum 18 points: 1–3 months earns up to 3 points; 3–12 months earns 5–7 points; 1–4 years earns 11–15 points; more than 4 years earns 18 points.

3. **EXPERIENCE:** Time of working in a specific employment. Maximum 8 points.

4. **OCCUPATIONAL DEMAND:** Maximum 10 points, based on need for the applicant's skills in Canada. (See Table 5.)

5. **ARRANGED EMPLOYMENT OR DESIGNATED OCCUPATION:** Maximum 10 points. Awarded when applicant has a guaranteed job offer that has been approved by a Canada Employment Centre or the occupation is included in the Designated Occupations List for the province where the applicant intends to live. (See Table 6.)

6. **AGE:** Maximum 10 points. Those 21–44 earn 10 points. 2 points are deducted for each year outside that age bracket.

7. **KNOWLEDGE OF ENGLISH AND FRENCH:** Maximum 15 points. Points are awarded on the basis of

Table 3
THE POINT SYSTEM: SELECTION CRITERIA
FOR INDEPENDENT IMMIGRANTS

Factor	Units of assessment	Notes
Education	12 maximum	
Specific vocational preparation	18 maximum	
Experience	8 maximum	0 units is an automatic processing bar, unless applicant has arranged employment
Occupation	10 maximum	
Arranged employment	10 maximum	
Demographic factor	10 maximum	
Age	10 maximum	10 units if 21 to 44; 2 units deducted for each year under 21 or over 44
Knowledge of English or French	15 maximum	
Personal suitability	10 maximum	
Total	**103**	
Pass mark	**70**	

Reprinted by permission of Employment and Immigration Canada.

the applicant's ability to speak, read or write one or both of Canada's official languages — fluently, well, or with difficulty.

8. **PERSONAL SUITABILITY:** Maximum 10 points. Awarded by a visa officer after a personal interview, and

based on applicant's adaptability, resourcefulness, motivation and initiative.

9. **DEMOGRAPHIC FACTOR:** Maximum 10 points, depending on high or low immigrant target level set for that year.

10. **BONUS POINTS:** A 5-point bonus is earned by those who have a relative in Canada. 45 bonus points are awarded to an investor or entrepreneur applicant; and 30 points to a self-employed applicant. Other bonus points apply solely to francophones wishing to settle in Quebec. Applications must be approved by the Quebec government's immigration services, as provided in the federal–provincial agreement on immigration.

Here are three examples of how the points may be applied:

APPLICANT A is a legal secretary, age 24, high school graduate, six months of secretarial training, three years' experience, fluent in English.

POINT ASSESSMENT: education, 12; specific vocational preparation, 11; experience, 6; occupational demand, 5; arranged employment, 0; demographic factor, 8; age, 10; language, 10; personal suitability, 10. Total points: 72. Visa granted.

APPLICANT B is a physician, age 50, with 20 years' experience, fairly good in French, weak in English.

(Because of provincial licensing requirements, this person cannot be assessed as a doctor, but he or she does have skills to qualify as a surgical assistant.)

POINT ASSESSMENT: education, 12; special vocational preparation, 7; experience, 8; occupational demand, 1; arranged employment, 0; demographic factor, 8; age, 0; language, 8; personal suitability, 8. Total points: 52. Visa denied.

APPLICANT C is an aircraft maintenance engineer, age 35, with a Grade 10 education, 15 years' experience, fluent in English. Some knowledge of French.

POINT ASSESSMENT: education, 10; special vocational preparation, 15; experience, 8; occupational demand, 0; arranged employment, 0; demographic factor, 8; age, 10; language, 10; personal suitability, 9. Total points: 70. Visa denied. Although the applicant merited 70 points, no points in both occupational demand and arranged employment means an automatic refusal.

CHAPTER THREE

The Family Class and Other Relatives

WHO IS A MEMBER OF THE FAMILY CLASS?

Family class applicants are sponsorable close family members. The point system does not apply to this category of immigrant. If they pass health and security requirements they are entitled to immigrant visas. The only other condition is that the sponsor post a guarantee for one to ten years, as required by Immigration, that sponsored family members will not fall on welfare in Canada.

Many relatives, including most brothers and sisters, are considered outside the family class. They cannot be sponsored. They must apply as independent immigrants and as such, must possess work skills that are in demand in Canada. They must obtain a minimum of 70 points in the selection criteria. If they have a relative in Canada they are awarded five bonus points. The former definition of "assisted relative" has been changed to eliminate the need for an undertaking of assistance in bringing to Canada relatives outside the family class.

SPONSORSHIP

A Canadian citizen, or a permanent resident at least 19 years old, may sponsor any number of the following close relatives or family class members:

1. A spouse.
2. A fiancé(e).
3. Dependent sons and daughters.
4. Parents and grandparents.
5. Brothers, sisters, nephews, nieces and grandchildren who are orphaned, unmarried and under the age of 19.

   The unmarried include those who are single, cohabiting, divorced, widowed, or whose marriage has been annulled.
6. A child you have adopted before he or she was 13 years of age — or a child you intend to adopt before he or she is 13 years of age.
7. Any relative, regardless of age or relationship, if you do not have any of the above sponsorable relatives or any relatives already living in Canada.

Sons and daughters are considered "sponsorable dependents" if they fit one of these three categories:

A. Under the age of 19 and unmarried. They must be unmarried when they apply as well as when the visa is issued.

B. Full-time students. They must have been studying at a college, university, or other educational institution, after turning 19 or marrying; they must be studying when they apply for their visas and when the visas are issued; and they must have been financially supported by their parents after turning 19 or marrying, if under the age of 19 when married. Students may interrupt their studies for up to 12 months and still be considered dependents.

C. Children with a disability. They must be supported financially by their parents, and be unable to support themselves because of the disability.

These regulations governing dependent children were introduced in 1992, and replaced regulations that permitted the sponsorship of never married children only, regardless of age. The previous policy had created unfair situations in which, for example, a self-supporting, 50-year-old bachelor qualified for sponsorship but a dependent, 18-year-old daughter who had been widowed, did not.

A marriage or divorce recognized both by the courts in the prospective immigrant's country of birth and in Canada (under provincial law), is automatically recognized for immigration purposes. Marriages and divorces legally performed or granted in other countries are not recognized by Immigration when such divorces or marriages would not be permitted according to the laws of Canada.

If an applicant has two wives, for example, only the first is considered his wife by immigration authorities. However, a second spouse may, at Immigration's discretion, be admitted to Canada on humanitarian and compassionate grounds, if Canadian authorities are satisfied that a family dependency has existed and continues to exist.

There is no provision in the law for the admission as a family dependent of a common-law spouse.

"Marriage by proxy" is recognized in Canada if it is valid under the law of the country in which the marriage ceremony is performed, provided there is no impediment to the marriage under Canadian law. Such cases must be investigated to establish a proxy marriage was entered into in good faith and not as a "marriage of convenience" to circumvent Canadian laws.

Special consideration is given to applications by relatives coming to Canada to work in small family businesses. The intent is to offer another opportunity for family reunification. The provision is not to be considered as another means of providing workers when no suitable Canadian applicant is available. It is intended to allow a Canadian resident to bring to Canada a relative, if it can be satisfactorily established that it is more sensible to employ a family member than a stranger already in Canada. It is conceded that family businesses demand a certain amount of trust which is not readily available when hiring non-relatives, and that in many cases family members are more committed to the success of the business.

The Canadian resident must provide the following: proof of ownership of the business; proof of personal income; a formal job offer addressed to the relatives; and a current financial statement for the business. A key criterion for approval of business applications is the viability of the business.

DNA FINGERPRINTING

Canadian immigration law recognizes for sponsorship purposes the relationship between a child born out of wedlock and his or her putative father. The key, however, is to produce satisfactory proof of the relationship with the person identified as the father. Until recently, this was almost impossible, but technological advances now allow us to use DNA genetic material to confirm parentage. The new technique analyses a person's deoxyribonucleic acid. Dubbed "DNA genetic fingerprinting," the test distinguishes a DNA pattern or profile which is unique to each person. All children inherit certain common DNA characteristics from their parents so that their DNA profile contains elements from each parent. These can be isolated and matched to determine that a parent–child relationship exists.

The DNA test is offered to the public at a cost of

about $900. The test requires that a blood sample be taken for analysis from both the mother and the father as well as the child. Tests involving one parent are not sufficiently conclusive. Each additional child to be tested will add an extra $240 to the fee. All costs are borne by the client seeking to establish the necessary relationship. The client is also responsible for ensuring that the parties involved make appointments for blood collections with the nearest Health and Welfare Canada doctor. They must also bring at least one recent photograph of themselves and an identification document bearing their photograph. The testing company will provide a blood test kit to the doctor taking the blood sample, which is then forwarded to the laboratory. Information about the DNA testing process may be obtained by writing to: Cellmark Diagnostics, 20271 Goldenrod Lane, German Town, Maryland 20874, U.S.A.

ADOPTION

Most Canadian residents who apply to sponsor a child whom they intend to adopt, do so in good faith. They may be childless couples yearning for a child to love and call their own; others may simply want to share their love and wealth by giving an orphaned child a home.

Too often, however, people apply to sponsor a nephew or niece they intend to adopt in Canada. It isn't that they want the child to be a member of the family, but because only through adoption would Immigration recognize the child as a family class member qualifying for sponsorship.

Immigration regulations permit sponsorship only to those adopted before age 13. This arbitrary cut-off was brought about because too many people were exploiting the adoption process. Many were adopting nieces and nephews as old as 16 and 17 so that they could gain permanent resident status.

The age 12 limit has caused heartache to many who raised children from infancy but did not go through legal channels to formally adopt them. A grandmother or an older sister who raised a child as her own, may be shocked to discover that the child can't immigrate to Canada with her, because she's not the child's legal parent.

Even when a child under the age of 13 is to be brought to Canada for adoption, the application is likely to be denied when the child has a living parent. Except in rare cases, the child must be an orphan or born out of wedlock and currently in the care of an institution. Child welfare authorities in Canada will not allow a child overseas to be plucked from the bosom of his or her mother simply because in Canada there's the promise of a good life that he or she could not otherwise hope to have.

Anyone in Canada thinking of adopting a young niece or nephew stands a better chance of having the child come to Canada if the adoption is processed through the courts in the child's own country. Provided the child is legally adopted before the age of 13, he or she is considered by Immigration to be a family dependent and may be readily sponsored.

MINIMUM INCOME LEVELS

The sponsor must satisfy Immigration that he or she can afford to provide accommodation and other basic needs to sponsored relatives until they become self-supporting in Canada. Sponsors should carefully consider what's involved to determine whether or not they are prepared to help their relatives at the expense of their established lifestyle.

Once a decision to sponsor a close family member is made, an application is submitted by the sponsor. If the sponsorship criteria are met, the file is then forwarded to the visa office handling applications from the sponsored relative's country. The process, which may take up to two years, involves an interview at the visa office and medical and security screenings.

Sponsors must show they have sufficient resources to provide accommodation for the relatives they wish to sponsor to this country. This requirement is waived in a spousal sponsorship.

If you want to sponsor a family class relative to come to Canada, you must pledge to be responsible for their care and shelter for a specific period. You have to prove you can afford to look after them.

If you fail to satisfy Immigration's minimum income level requirement, which depends on the number of people being sponsored and other factors, other eligible family members may sign as co-sponsors. The number of people who may be sponsored is directly linked to Immigration's regularly adjusted minimum income levels. The more people to be sponsored, the higher the income bracket required of the sponsor. Another important requirement is to provide acceptable proof of relationship between the Canadian sponsor and his or her relative abroad. Immigration authorities assess a prospective sponsor's resources against an income bracket adjusted to the number of people being sponsored, the sponsor's family dependents and financial obligations, and the sponsored relatives' intended final destination. The income level applying to large urban centres is much higher than that for smaller centres and rural areas. Income levels are adjusted from time to time to reflect inflation. In Toronto, where approximately 25 per cent of all immigrants to Canada tend to settle, a sponsor with no dependents must have an income of about $25,000 a year to qualify as a sponsor for his or her parents and a sibling. (See Table 4.) It is against the law to give false and misleading information to immigration authorities. If a lie is detected, the visa process is halted and criminal charges may be laid.

SPONSORSHIP DENIALS AND APPEALS

Canadian citizens and permanent residents have the right to bring to Canada close family members, provided sponsorship conditions are fully met by both the sponsor and the sponsored. This means the family member must pass the routine medical examination and police clearance requirement; and the sponsor must meet the minimum income level required for sponsorship, depending on the number of relatives being sponsored. A rejection may be appealed to the Appeals

Table 4
LOW INCOME CUT-OFF OF FAMILY UNITS

Size of Family Unit	Size of Area of Residence				
	A 500,000 and over	**B** 100,000 – 499,999	**C** 30,000 – 99,999	**D** Less than – 30,000**	**E** Rural Areas
1 person	$14,951	$13,132	$12,829	$11,695	$10,179
2 persons	$20,266	$17,802	$17,390	$15,852	$13,799
3 persons	$25,761	$22,626	$22,103	$20,149	$17,539
4 persons	$29,661	$26,049	$25,449	$23,200	$20,192
5 persons	$32,406	$28,462	$27,805	$25,347	$22,062
6 persons	$35,177	$30,893	$30,180	$27,512	$23,947
7 persons	$37,833	$33,230	$32,463	$29,593	$25,757
For Each Additional Person	$2,710	$2,380	$2,330	$2,120	$1,850

** Includes non-metropolitan cities (with a population between 15,000 and 30,000) and small urban areas (under 15,000).
Reprinted by permission of Employment and Immigration Canada.

Division of the Immigration and Refugee Board. If the board rules in your favour, it will likely also direct the visa office to reconsider the application to reflect the board's findings. The board may find no fault in the immigration department's decision, but nonetheless may allow sponsorship on humanitarian and compassionate grounds.

CHAPTER FOUR

Refugees

CONVENTION REFUGEES

Today, as many as 80 million people are on the move throughout the world in search of a country to call home. Many are seeking a more politically and economically stable country in a bid to build for themselves and their families a better lifestyle. Others are seeking sanctuary in the West, where they will be free from wars, political turmoil or ethnic strife. Hundreds of thousands languish in refugee camps in southeast Asia and other parts of the world, longing for visas to Canada or any other Western country that might accept them.

The federal government annually airlifts to Canada a predetermined number of refugees from scattered parts of the world. Those brought to Canada under the federal program are provided with shelter, accommodation and training at Canadian taxpayers' expense. In addition, groups of Canadian residents, including church groups and ethnic community organizations, may also sign agreements with the federal government so that they may sponsor individual refugees. Sponsors assume financial responsibility for such refugees during their first year in Canada. Currently, about 33,000 refugees are brought to Canada each year. Another 25,000 are granted refugee status from within Canada.

A Convention Refugee is a person who fits the United Nations' definition of refugee, namely, "a person who, by reason of a well-founded fear of persecution for reasons of race, religion, nationality, membership in a particular social group or political opinion, (a) is outside the country of his nationality and is unable or, by reason of that fear, is unwilling to avail himself of the protection of that country, or (b) not having a country or nationality, is outside the country of his former habitual residence and is unable, or by reason of such fear, is unwilling to return to that country."

Although wife assault does not fall within the U.N. definition of refugee, nonetheless, the Refugee Board may consider claims by abused women based on fear of persecution because of sex. Such consideration on humanitarian grounds applies mostly to women from countries where the law is deemed to provide inadequate protection for battered women.

Canada is a signatory to the 1951 United Nations' Geneva Convention and the 1967 Protocol Relating to the Status of Refugees. The Immigration Act, in accordance with the Convention definition of refugee, excludes from protection people who have committed war crimes, serious non-political crimes and "acts contrary to the purposes and principles of the United Nations."

Claiming refugee status from within Canada

Canada has long been regarded as a generous country offering sanctuary to tens of thousands of refugees. Indeed, Canada has the highest refugee acceptance rate in the world. In 1986, the United Nations recognized Canada's humanitarian efforts by awarding the people of Canada the Nansen Medal. This generosity in the eyes of the world has spawned an increasing flow of visitors and other individuals, who apply in large numbers each year for refugee status from within Canada.

In the past three years more than 100,000 people have claimed refugee status after coming to Canada. Most had come to Canada under the guise of visitors. More than 23,000 of them, however, arrived with no travel documents or proper identification. Many have unfounded claims of persecution. They make a mockery of Canada's refugee system in their bid to remain in Canada for economic reasons. The new immigration law empowers immigration authorities to fingerprint and photograph refugee claimants. Immigration authorities may turn back or deport people known to belong to criminal or terrorist organizations, albeit they may have no criminal record.

THE REFUGEE STATUS DETERMINATION SYSTEM

The system is designed to meet both Canada's international obligations under the Geneva Convention and the provisions of Canada's Charter of Rights and Freedoms.

Refugee claimants are given every opportunity to show they have a credible basis for claiming such status in Canada. They are given time and assistance to present their case and to ensure that all facts relevant to their claim are on record.

The refugee determination process involves a single-level hearing before an independent, two-member Immigration Refugee Board. In most cases, a positive decision by either of the two board members is enough to determine that the claimant is a refugee. Indeed, the benefit of the doubt applies in most cases. However, a unanimous decision is required when considering claimants who come to Canada without satisfactory identification, or who visit their countries of origin while their claims are pending.

This is also the case, under certain conditions, for people coming from countries such as the United States, where they could have made a claim for refugee status and had a fair hearing. However, as a rule, those from the U.S. and such countries, do not have access to the Refugee Board. Neither do those making a repeat refugee claim less than 90 days after a previous claim was rejected; those considered to be serious criminals by an adjudicator; and, to eliminate "asylum shopping," anyone already recognized as a refugee.

The new regulations permit the claimant's spouse and dependent children, who may have been left behind in their country of origin, to be granted permanent resident status at the same time. Previously, they could only be sponsored to Canada after the claimant gained permanent resident status, thus delaying the family's reunion for two or three years. Medical inadmissibility criteria are waived for accepted refugees and their immediate family members. Immigration

Refugee Board decisions may be appealed to the Trial Division of the Federal Court. However, access to the court will only be allowed if a trial division judge identifies the case as involving a serious question of law.

When the board finds a claim to be manifestly unfounded, removal of the claimant from Canada may take place before the review is held. This may occur after a seven-day wait, to allow the claimant to consult legal counsel. If the Federal Court reverses the decision, the claimant will be invited to return to Canada at the government's expense.

Claimants are generally released pending the outcome of the decision. However, immigration authorities are empowered to detain those they believe may pose a threat to Canadian society, or are deemed likely to skip future hearings and remain illegally in Canada.

Canada's Immigration Act provides for the removal of refugee status when a return to one's country is no longer considered dangerous. However, in most cases, those whose claims are deemed to have a credible basis are routinely given the green light to apply for permanent resident status, and subsequently to become Canadian citizens.

FILING A CLAIM

Every claimant has the right to counsel. A lawyer, friend, relative or other individual may help a claimant present his or her case.

Interpreters and translators are provided to help claimants present a full and complete story documenting their fear of returning to their countries. A claim will not be considered if filed by a person who has refugee status elsewhere, or has already been considered in Canada not to be a Convention Refugee, or who has failed to leave Canada as ordered by an adjudicator at a previous inquiry during which no claim for refugee status had been made.

Those who gain approval may apply for permanent resident status. Dependents are included in the application, but all must pass normal background checks.

CHAPTER FIVE

Independent Immigrants

WHO IS AN INDEPENDENT IMMIGRANT?

Entrepreneurs, investors, self-employed people and others having skills in demand in Canada all fit into the independent immigrant class. They must meet the criteria established by the point system of immigrant selection. Normally they must obtain 70 points based on various factors ranging from age and education to knowledge of English or French, or both, and the need for the applicant's training and work skills in this country.

As explained in Chapter 3, those who fail to obtain the required points may obtain an additional five points if they have a relative in Canada.

Those who do not obtain at least one point in the work experience factor must have an arranged job in

Canada, or be qualified to accept employment in a designated occupation — in an area of Canada identified as having a shortage of workers in that occupation. An arranged job must have the approval of a Canada Employment Centre, that is, confirmation that the prospective employer cannot find Canadian workers willing and able to take the job.

THE EMPLOYMENT FACTOR

Obtaining approval of a job offer isn't easy because Canada Employment Centres are required to make such vacancies available to Canadian workers first. The Canada Employment and Immigration Commission must be satisfied that there are no Canadian workers available and willing to do the work. In some cases, when workers are not readily available locally, jobless workers from other parts of Canada may be offered the chance to relocate where the jobs are available.

Only when vacancies are hard to fill does it become easy for qualified foreign workers to obtain work permits or landed immigrant status. The assessment of the Canadian labour market need is determined by Canada Employment Centres, but final approval rests with immigration authorities and visa officers abroad.

A visa is granted when Canadian workers are not available and the training of Canadians for such work is not considered feasible. Of course, the assessment involves a time-consuming search for Canadian workers, an investigation into whether the job is genuine, or whether a labour strike is involved, working conditions, expected duration of the work period and the feasibility of training Canadians for the work. The application form must be submitted by the employer. Such an approved employment requirement does not apply to sponsored family class relatives and independent immigrants who have work skills needed in Canada. Universities are not required to advertise or otherwise consider applications from Canadian academics before recruiting foreign applicants.

Priests and other religious personnel

Clergymen, priests, lay personnel and members of religious orders do not have to obtain job offer approval by a Canada Employment Centre, provided the intention is to perform religious duties only in Canada. This includes preaching of doctrine, liturgy and spiritual counselling.

During the application procedure the Canadian religious organization must provide the offer of employment to the religious worker. But the visa office is not required to have it confirmed by immigration authorities in Canada, if the office has sufficient information to believe the applicant will be adequately funded.

GENERAL AND DESIGNATED OCCUPATIONS

A list of "general occupations" for which prospective immigrants may obtain up to 10 points, and the "designated occupations" by which immigrants may gain an additional 10 points without the need of an approved job offer, are announced by the Minister of Immigration at the beginning of each year. (See Tables 5 and 6.) The occupations lists reflect the labour shortages in Canada. Immigration officials draft the lists after extensive consultations with government and industry experts.

The federal government's separate listing of designated occupations is aimed at filling the needs of provinces that do not get a fair share of the qualified skilled workers coming to Canada. Thus, prospective immigrants having skills in designated occupations and willing to settle in communities where they're needed get priority consideration by visa officers.

Approval may well hinge on whether a set target of skilled workers in a specific occupation has been attained for that year, in the province of intended settlement. Professionals often must satisfy standards established by professional licensing bodies before they may continue in those careers in Canada.

The general occupations list and the designated occupations list both promote the integration of people who may quickly become gainfully employed and established in Canada, while also providing employers with needed skilled workers.

The general occupations list contains more than 100 broad occupational groups covering a wide range of work skills. In the designated occupations program, provinces are encouraged to determine their specific needs after consultations with labour groups and the private sector. Participating provinces may recruit skilled workers directly from abroad. Applicants with arranged employment in designated occupations are awarded an automatic 20 points — 10 because they have needed skills and another 10 because they have jobs waiting for them.

Table 5
GENERAL OCCUPATIONS LIST

Occupational title	Points
MANAGEMENT AND ADMINISTRATION	
ACCOUNTANTS, AUDITORS AND OTHER FINANCIAL OFFICERS	3
ORGANIZATION AND METHODS ANALYSTS	3
PERSONNEL AND RELATED OFFICERS	
Labour-Relations Specialist	3
Personnel Officer	3
Employment Recruiter	3
Outplacement Relocation Specialist	3
Occupational Analyst	3
Financial-Aids Officer	3
Counsellor, Pre-Retirement	3
Employment Interviewer	3
PURCHASING OFFICERS AND BUYERS, EXCEPT WHOLESALE AND RETAIL TRADE	I
INSPECTORS AND REGULATORY OFFICERS, NON-GOVERNMENT	
Safety Inspector	5
Insurance Inspector, Loss-Prevention	5
Safety Co-ordinator	5
Traffic Inspector	5
Radiation-Contamination Monitor	5
Service-Station Inspector	5
Acreage-Quota-Assignment Officer	5
Dining-Service Inspector	5
Inspector, Travel Accommodation	5
Gas-Customer-Liaison Agent	5
Ammunition-Safety Inspector	5
OCCUPATIONS RELATED TO MANAGEMENT AND ADMINISTRATION, not elsewhere classified	
Agent	I
Campaign Consultant	I
Tour Operator	I
Travel Agent	I
Co-ordinator, Tourism	I

Table 5 continued

Occupational title	Points
Public-Relations Agent	I
Interpretation-Visitor Services Coordinator	I
Community Arts Coordinator	I
Industrial-Development Representative	I
Sales-Promotion Administrator	I
Technical-Service Consultant	I
Management-Seminar Leader	I
Corporate Secretary	I
Quantity Surveyor	I
Administrative Officer	I
Corporate Planner	I
Contracts Administrator	I
Conference and Meeting Planner	I
Stations-Relations Administrator	I
Property Administrator	I
Food-and-Beverage Controller	I
Freight-Traffic Consultant	I
Cost Estimator	I
Graphoanalyst	I
SCIENCES	
CHEMISTS	I
GEOLOGISTS AND	
RELATED OCCUPATIONS	I
PHYSICISTS	I
PHYSICAL SCIENCES TECHNOLOGISTS AND	
TECHNICIANS	
Chemical Technologist	I
Forest-Products Technologist	I
Geological Technologist	I
Geophysical Technologist	I
Laboratory Physical Sciences Technologist	I
Textile Technologist	I
Holographic Technician	I
Assayer	I

Table 5 continued

Occupational title	Points
Water-Purification Technician	I
Chemical Technician, Heavy Water Plant and Nuclear-Generating Station	I
Chemical Technician	I
Geological Technician	I
Hydrology Technician	I
Meteorological Technician	I
Laboratory Physical Sciences Technician	I
Textile Technician	I
Geophysical-Equipment Operator, Airborne	I
Geophycial Technician	I
AGRICULTURISTS AND RELATED SCIENTISTS	I
FORESTER	I
ARCHITECTURE AND ENGINEERING	
ARCHITECTS	I
CHEMICAL ENGINEERS	5
CIVIL ENGINEERS	
Materials and Testing Engineer	5
Structural-Design Engineer	5
Civil Engineer, General	5
Airport Engineer	5
Buildings and Bridge Engineer	5
Coastal Engineer	5
Ocean Engineer	5
Environmental Engineer	5
Highway Engineer	5
Irrigation and Drainage Engineer	5
Pipeline Engineer	5
Railway Engineer	5
Soil Engineer	5
Water-Resources Engineer	5
ELECTRICAL ENGINEERS	
Design and Development Engineer, Electrical and Electronic	5

Table 5 continued

Occupational title	Points
Research Engineer, Electrical and Electronic	5
Electrical Engineer, General	5
Electronic Engineer, General	5
Audio Engineer	5
Distribution Engineer	5
Electrical and Electronic Aerospace Engineer	5
Electrical-Equipment Engineer	5
Electrical-Systems-Planning Engineer	5
Illuminating Engineer	5
Plant Engineer, Electrical	5
Signal Engineer	5
Telephone Engineer	5
Transmission Engineer	5
INDUSTRIAL ENGINEERS	5
MECHANICAL ENGINEERS	
Power Engineer, Mechanical	5
Tool Engineer	5
Mechanical Engineer, General	5
Automotive Engineer	5
Heating-Ventilating and Air-Conditioning Engineer	5
Lubrication Engineer	5
Mechanical Engineer, Gas Utilization	5
Propulsion Engineer, Aerospace Vehicles	5
Refrigeration Engineer	5
METALLURGICAL ENGINEERS	5
MINING ENGINEERS	5
PETROLEUM ENGINEERS	5
AEROSPACE ENGINEERS	
Aerospace Engineer, Design and Development	5
Aerospace Engineer, Mass Properties	5
Aerospace Engineer, General	5
Aerospace Engineer, Flight-Test	5
Aerospace Engineer, Materials and Processes	5
Aerospace Engineer, Flight Operations	5
Aerospace Engineer, Flight Support	5

Table 5 continued

Occupational title	Points
NUCLEAR ENGINEERS	5
ARCHITECTS AND ENGINEERS, not elsewhere classified	
Agricultural Engineer	5
Ceramics Engineer	5
Marine Engineer	5
Ship-Construction Engineer	5
Biomedical Engineer, Research and Development	5
Biomedical Engineer, Clinical	5
Gas and Steam-Distribution Engineer	5
Cryogenics Engineer	5
Geological Engineer	5
Forest Engineer	5
Welding Engineer	5
Fire-Prevention Engineer	5
Traffic Engineer	5
Corrosion Engineer	5
Logging Engineer, Oil Well	5
SURVEYOR	1
ARCHITECTURAL AND ENGINEERING TECHNOLOGISTS AND TECHNICIANS	
Aerospace-Engineering Technologist	1
Architectural Technologist	1
Chemical Engineering Technologist	1
Civil-Engineering Technologist	1
Electrical-Engineering Technologist	1
Electronic-Engineering Technologist	1
Industrial-Engineering Technologist	1
Marine-Engineering Technologist	1
Mechanical-Engineering Technologist	1
Metallurgical-Engineering Technologist	1
Mining-Engineering Technologist	1
Nuclear-Engineering Technologist	1
Nuclear Technologist	1
Petrochemical-Engineering Technologist	1
Manufacturing Cost Estimator	1

Table 5 continued

Occupational title	Points
Mould Designer	1
Aerospace-Engineering Technician	1
Agricultural-Engineering Technician	1
Chemical-Engineering Technician	1
Civil-Engineering Technician	1
Drilling-Fluid Technician, Offshore Drilling Rig	1
Electrical-Engineering Technician	1
Metrology Technician	1
Electronic-Engineering Technician	1
Geological-Engineering Technician	1
Industrial-Engineering Technician	1
Marine-Engineering Technician	1
Mechanical-Engineering Technician	1
Metallurgical-Engineering Technician	1
Mining-Engineering Technician	1
Nuclear-Engineering Technician	1
Petrochemical-Engineering Technician	1
Petroleum-Engineering Technician	1
Pollution Control Technician	1
OTHER OCCUPATIONS IN ARCHITECTURE AND ENGINEERING, not elsewhere classified	
Photogrammetist	5
Remote Sensing Technician	5
Aerial-Photograph Analyst	5
Stereoplotter	5
MATHEMATICS AND COMPUTER SCIENCE	
MATHEMATICIANS, STATISTICIANS AND ACTUARIES	1
SYSTEMS ANALYSTS, COMPUTER PROGRAMMERS AND RELATED OCCUPATIONS	10
SOCIAL SCIENCES AND RELATED FIELDS	
ECONOMISTS	1

Table 5 continued

Occupational title	Points
PSYCHOLOGISTS	3
SOCIAL WORKERS	
Social-Work Supervisor	5
Community-Organization Worker	5
Parole Officer	5
Probation Officer	5
Social Worker	5
Social Worker, Case Work	5
Social Worker, Group	5
Counsellor, Addiction	5
OCCUPATIONS IN WELFARE AND COMMUNITY SERVICES	
Child-Care Worker	5
Community-Development Worker	5
Teaching Homemaker	5
Half-Way House Supervisor	5
Geriatric-Activities Aide	5
Detention-Home Worker	5
OCCUPATIONS IN SOCIAL WORK AND RELATED FIELDS, not elsewhere classified	
Research Officer, Social Welfare	5
Student-Activities Adviser	5
OCCUPATIONS IN LAW AND JURISPRUDENCE, not elsewhere classified	
Law Clerk	1
Patent Searcher	1
Contract Clerk	1
Land-Titles Clerk	1
Title Examiner	1
LIBRARIANS, ARCHIVISTS AND CONSERVATORS	3
OTHER OCCUPATIONS IN SOCIAL SCIENCES, AND RELATED FIELDS, not elsewhere classified	
Rehabilitation Specialist	5
Counsellor, Rehabilitation	5

Table 5 continued

Occupational title	Points
Counsellor, Marriage	5
Counsellor, Attendance	5
Hypnotherapist	5
INSTRUCTORS AND TRAINING OFFICERS, not elsewhere classified	
Instructor, Airline Pilot	1
Training Specialist, Computers	1
Flying Instructor	1
Flying Instructor, Helicopter	1
Sewing Instructor	1
Ground-School Instructor	1
Instructor, Police	1
Instructor, Flight Attendant	1
Training Representative	1
Instructor, Auto Driving	1
MEDICINE AND HEALTH	
VETERINARIANS	1
PHYSIOTHERAPISTS, OCCUPATIONAL AND OTHER THERAPISTS	
Audiologist	10
Speech Pathologist	10
Clinical Occupational Therapy Specialist	10
Community Occupational Therapist	10
Occupational Therapist	10
Physiotherapist	10
Remedial Gymnast	10
NURSING, THERAPY AND RELATED ASSISTING OCCUPATIONS, not elsewhere classified	
Surgical Assistant	1
Operating Room Assistant	1
Music Therapist	1

Table 5 continued

Occupational title	Points
Recreational Therapist	1
Art Therapist	1
Dance Therapist	1
PHARMACISTS	1
DIETICIANS AND NUTRITIONISTS	1
RADIOLOGICAL TECHNICIANS	
Diagnostic Medical Sonographer	5
Nuclear-Medicine Technician	5
Diagnostic-Radiological Technician	5
Radiotherapy Technician	10
MEDICAL LABORATORY TECHNOLOGISTS AND TECHNICIANS	
Biochemistry Technologist	5
Cytogenetics Technologist	5
Cytotechnologist	5
Electron Microscopy Technologist	5
Histology Technologist	5
Medical-Laboratory Technologist	5
Immunology Technologist	5
Immunohematology Technologist	5
Microbiology Technologist	5
Laboratory Technician, Veterinary	5
DENTURISTS, DENTAL HYGIENISTS, DENTAL ASSISTANTS AND DENTAL TECHNICIANS	
Dental Hygienist	5
Denturist	1
Dental Technician, General	1
Dental Ceramist	1
Dental Technician, Crown and Bridge	1
Dental Technician, Metal	1
Orthodontic Technician	1
Denture Setter	1
Framework Finisher, Dentures	1

Table 5 continued

Occupational title	Points
Moulder, Bench	1
Orthodontic-Band Maker	1
OTHER OCCUPATIONS IN MEDICINE AND HEALTH, not elsewhere classified	
Prosthetist-Orthotist	10
Respiratory Technologist	10
Electroencephalographic Technician	10
DESIGN, PUBLICATION AND RELATED FIELDS	
PRODUCT AND INTERIOR DESIGNERS	
Exhibition and Display Designer	1
Interior Designer and Decorator	1
Furniture Designer	1
Set Designer	1
Stained-Glass Artist	1
Fur Designer	1
Garment Designer	1
Industrial-Products Designer	1
Shoe Designer	1
Textile Designer	1
Commercial-Design Artist	1
Package Designer	1
Pottery Designer	1
Women's Fashion Designer	1
Designer, Paper Securities	1
Embroidery Designer	1
Handbag Designer	1
Sign Designer	1
Office-Space Planner	1
ADVERTISING AND ILLUSTRATING ARTISTS	3
PRODUCERS AND DIRECTORS, PERFORMING AND AUDIOVISUAL ARTS	3
WRITERS AND EDITORS, PUBLICATION	3
TRANSLATORS AND INTERPRETERS	1

Table 5 continued

Occupational title	Points
CLERICAL AND RELATED OCCUPATIONS	
SECRETARIES AND STENOGRAPHERS	
Secretary	5
Executive Secretary	5
Legal Secretary	5
Medical Secretary	5
Court Reporter	5
Technical Secretary	5
Bookkeeper	I
INSURANCE, BANK AND	
OTHER FINANCE CLERKS	
General Clerk, Insurance	I
Policy-Change Clerk	I
Property and Equipment Insurance Clerk	I
Special-Endorsement Clerk	I
Utility Clerk, Bank	I
Foreign-Remittance Clerk	I
Reserves Clerk	
ELECTRONIC DATA-PROCESSING	
EQUIPMENT OPERATORS	
Computer Operator	I
Computerized-Information Processor	I
PRODUCTION CLERKS	
Production Co-ordinator	I
Material Co-ordinator	I
Motor Vehicle Repair Co-ordinator	I
Control Clerk, Advertising	I
STOCK CLERKS AND RELATED OCCUPATIONS	
Production-Supply Clerk	3
Storekeeper, Drilling Rig	3
ADJUSTERS, CLAIM	
Claim Adjuster	3
Service Representative	3
Claim Examiner	3
Marine-Cargo Surveyor	3

Table 5 continued

Occupational title	Points
OTHER CLERICAL AND RELATED OCCUPATIONS, not elsewhere classified	
Copy Cutter	3
Bus-Transportation-Service Co-ordinator	3
Suggestion-Program Clerk	3
Engineering Clerk	3
SALES OCCUPATIONS	
TECHNICAL SALES OCCUPATIONS AND RELATED ADVISERS	I
COMMERCIAL TRAVELLERS	
Manufacturers' Agent	I
Pharmaceutical Representative	I
Sales Representative, Textbooks	I
Sales Representative, Canvas Products	I
Sales Representative, Commerical and Industrial Equipment and Supplies	I
Sales Representative, Food Products	I
Sales Representative, Wine, Beer and Spirits	I
Sales Representative, Garments and other Textile Products	I
Sales Representative, Motor Vehicles and Equipment	I
Sales Representative, Petroleum Products	I
Sales Representative, Plastic Products	I
Sales Representative, Pulp and Paper Products	I
Sales Representative, Rubber Products	I
SALES WORKERS, COMMODITIES, not elsewhere classified	
Salesperson, Motor Vehicles	3
Leasing Representative, Motor Vehicles	3
Salesperson, Sewing Machines	3
Salesperson, Computers	3
Salesperson, Hearing Aids	3
Salesperson, Livestock	3
Salesperson, Art	3

Table 5 continued

Occupational title	Points
Salesperson, Musical Instruments and Supplies	3
Automotive Partsperson	3
Salesperson, Wood Burning Appliances	3
Industrial Engines and Equipment Partsperson	3
Salesperson, Parts	3
ADVERTISING SALES OCCUPATIONS	3
BUYERS, WHOLESALE AND RETAIL TRADE	1
OTHER SKILLED OCCUPATIONS, INCLUDING MECHANICS AND REPAIRERS	
GRAIN-ELEVATOR MANAGER	1
FIRE-FIGHTING OCCUPATIONS	
Fire-Fighter, Crash	3
Fire-Fighter	3
PROTECTIVE SERVICE OCCUPATIONS, not elsewhere classified	
Conservation Officer	3
CHEFS AND COOKS	
Chef-Cook, General	10
Head Chef	10
Banquet Chef	10
Cook, Small Establishment	10
Chef, Patissier	10
Chef, Saucier	10
Chef, Rotisseur	10
Cook, Domestic	10
Chef, Garde-Manger	10
Chef, Entremetier	10
Caterer	10
Cook, Institution	10
Working Sous-Chef	10
Cook, Kosher Foods	10
Cook, Foreign Foods	10
Cook, First	10
Cook, Therapeutic Diet	10

Table 5 continued

Occupational title	Points
Cook, Camp	10
BARBERS, HAIRDRESSERS AND RELATED OCCUPATIONS	
Make-Up Artist	1
Image Consultant	1
Barber	1
Hairdresser	1
MINING AND QUARRYING: CUTTING, HANDLING AND LOADING OCCUPATIONS	
Power-Shovel Operator	1
Continuous-Mining-Machine Operator	1
Longwall Coal-Shearer Operator	1
Cutting-Machine Operator	1
MOULDING, COREMAKING AND METAL CASTING OCCUPATIONS	
Moulder, Bench	10
DISTILLING, SUBLIMING AND CARBONIZING OCCUPATIONS, CHEMICALS AND RELATED MATERIALS	
Petroleum-Process Operator	1
SLAUGHTERING AND MEAT CUTTING, CANNING, CURING AND PACKING OCCUPATIONS	
Butcher, All-Round	1
Skinner, Animal	1
Butcher	1
TOOL-AND-DIE-MAKING OCCUPATIONS	
Tool and Die Maker	1
Mould Maker	1
Diamond-Tool Maker	1
Die Maker, Bench, Stamping	1
Die Maker, Wire-Drawing	1
Die Sinker, Bench	1
Tool Maker, Bench	1
Carbide-Tool Maker	1
Die Finisher	1

Table 5 continued

Occupational title	Points
Die Maker, Jewellery	1
Extrusion-Die Template Maker	1
MACHINIST AND MACHINING-TOOL SETTING-UP OCCUPATIONS	
Machine-Tool Set-Up Operator	1
Machinist, General	1
INSPECTING AND TESTING OCCUPATIONS, METAL MACHINING	
Inspector, Tool and Gauge	5
Inspector, Machine Shop	5
Gear Inspector	5
Propeller Inspector	5
FORGING OCCUPATIONS	
Die Setter	5
Blacksmith	5
Power-Hammer Operator	5
PATTERNMAKERS AND MOULDMAKERS	
Patternmaker, Wood	5
Model Maker, Wood	5
Model Maker, Last	5
Sample Maker, Jewellery	5
Model Maker	5
Patternmaker, Metal	5
Loftsman/woman	5
Model Maker, Jewellery	5
Patternmaker, Metal Furniture	5
Patternmaker, Pantographic Machine	5
Patternmaker, Envelopes	5
Template Maker	5
Patternmaker, Hat	5
Patternmaker, Plaster	5
Model-and-Mould Maker, Concrete Products	5
Mould Maker	5
Tire-Mould Repairer	5
Jig-and-Form Repairer	5

Table 5 continued

Occupational title	Points
ELECTRICAL AND RELATED EQUIPMENT INSTALLING AND REPAIRING OCCUPATIONS, not elsewhere classified	
Electrical Repairer	1
Electrician, Automotive	1
Refrigeration Mechanic	1
Repairer, Electric Motor	1
Rig Electrician	1
Electrician, Aircraft	1
Electrician, Marine Equipment	1
Electrician, Rail Transport	1
Repairer, Electrical Instruments	1
Wirer and Repairer, Office Machines	1
Repairer, Refrigeration Unit	1
Installer and Repairer, Automatic-Pinsetting Machine	1
Installer-Servicer, Dental Equipment	1
Repairer, Air-Conditioner	1
Repairer, Electric Tool	1
Repairer, Storage Battery	1
ELECTRONIC AND RELATED EQUIPMENT INSTALLING AND REPAIRING OCCUPATIONS, not elsewhere classified	
Electronic Technician, Drilling Rig	1
CADD/CAM Repair Technician	1
Robotics Technician	1
Computer Equipment Repair Technician	1
Process-Control Equipment Repairer	1
Installer, Aircraft-Electronic-Equipment	1
Repairer, Electronic-Equipment	1
Installer and Repairer, Audio-Visual Equipment	1
Repairer, Radio-Communication Equipment	1
Video Equipment Repairer	1
Electronic Music Equipment Repairer	1
Cellular Telephone Installer	1
Repairer, Television-Studio Equipment	1

Table 5 continued

Occupational title	Points
Security Alarm Installer	1
Installer and Repairer, Public-Address System	1
Repairer, Nucleonic-Controller	1
Electronic Games Repairer	1
Repairer, Automated-Processing Equipment	1
Satellite Antenna Installer	1
Hearing Aid Repairer	1
Production Repairer	1
SHOEMAKING AND REPAIRING OCCUPATIONS	
Shoemaker, Custom	1
Shoe Repairer	1
UPHOLSTERERS	
Upholsterer, All Around	1
Custom Upholsterer	1
Patternmaker-and-Upholsterer, Aircraft	1
Vehicle-Upholstery Repairer	1
AIRCRAFT MECHANICS AND REPAIRERS	
Aircraft Maintenance Engineer	1
Aircraft Mechanic	1
Aircraft-Accessories Mechanic	1
INDUSTRIAL, FARM AND CONSTRUCTION MACHINERY MECHANICS AND REPAIRERS	
Printing-Machinery Mechanic	10
Heavy-Duty-Equipment Mechanic	10
Loom Fixer	10
Machine Fixer, Textile	10
Millwright	10
Ore-Processing-Equipment Repairer	10
Powerhouse Repairer	10
Mechanical Maintainer, Nuclear-Generating Station and Heavy Water Plant	10
Metalworking-Machinery Mechanic	10
Chemical-Process-Equipment Mechanic	10
Plastics Processing Equipment Mechanic	10
Bakery-Machinery Mechanic	10

Table 5 continued

Occupational title	Points
Boilerhouse Repairer	10
Forge-Shop-Machinery Repairer	10
Gum-Wrapping-Machine Mechanic	10
Tannery-Machinery Repairer	10
Packaging-Machine Mechanic	10
Quilting-Machine Fixer	10
Maintenance Mechanic, Compressed-Gas-Plant	10
Oil-Tool Repairer	10
Powder-Line Repairer	10
Treatment-Plant Mechanic	10
Farm-Equipment Installer	10
Welding-Equipment Installer	10
Oven-Equipment Repairer	10
Sewing-Machine Mechanic	10
Ammunition-Assembling-Machine Adjuster	10
Carton-Forming-Machine Repairer	10
Fibreglass-Forming-Machine Repairer	10
Laundry-Machine Mechanic	10
Record-Process-Equipment Repairer	10
Seamer-Machine Repairer	10
Tobacco-Machine Adjuster	10
Card Grinder	10
Shearing-Machine Fixer	10
Machine-Clothing Replacer	10
Roll Builder	10
Dairy-Equipment Repairer	10
Farm-Equipment Mechanic	10
Mine-Hoist Repairer	10
Crane Repairer	10
Conveyor Repairer	10
Construction-Equipment Mechanic	10
Diesel Mechanic	10
INSPECTING AND TESTING OCCUPATIONS, EQUIPMENT REPAIR, not elsewhere classified	
Aircraft Inspector, Repair	3

Table 5 continued

Occupational title	Points
Locomotive Inspector	3
Aircraft-Hydraulics Tester	3
Railway-Car Inspector	3
Wheel-and-Axle Inspector	3
Maintenance Analyst	3
Inspector, Heavy Equipment	3
Gas Meter Tester	3
Aircraft Engine Tester	3
Automotive Vehicle Tester	3
Inspector and Tester, Meteorological Equipment	3
WATCH REPAIRERS	I
PRECISION-INSTRUMENT MECHANICS AND REPAIRERS	
Aircraft-Instrument Mechanic	5
Instrument Repairer	5
Camera Repairer	5
Photo-Finishing-Equipment Repairer	5
Gas-Meter Repairer	5
Gyroscope Repairer	5
MECHANICS AND REPAIRERS, EXCEPT ELECTRICAL, not elsewhere classified	
Gunsmith	5
Repairer, Small Engines	5
Locksmith	5
Pneumatic-Tool Repairer	5
Pneumatic-Tube Repairer	5
Hydraulic-Unit Repairer	5
Pneumatic-Unit Tester and Repairer	5
Scale Mechanic	5
Air-Compressor Repairer	5
ELECTRICAL POWER LINE WORKERS AND RELATED OCCUPATIONS	
Line Maintainer, Emergency Service	5
Line Repairer	5
Line Maintainer	5

Table 5 continued

Occupational title	Points
Cable Installer-Repairer	5
WIRE COMMUNICATIONS AND RELATED EQUIPMENT INSTALLING AND REPAIRING OCCUPATIONS	
Central-Office-Equipment Repairer	3
Rural-Telephone Maintainer	3
Electrician, Communications Equipment	3
Private-Branch-Exchange Repairer	3
Station Repairer	3
Telegraph-Equipment Repairer	3
Cable Installer	3
Line Installer-Repairer	3
Repairer, Shop	3
Central-Office-Equipment Installer	3
Private-Branch-Exchange Installer	3
Telephone-Station Installer	3
Telecommunications-Equipment Installer	3
Cable-Television Installer	3
INSPECTING AND TESTING OCCUPATIONS	
Electrical Wiring Inspector	5
Cable Tester	5
Tester and Regulator	5
Exchange Tester	5
Terminal and Repeater Tester	5
Transmission Tester	5
Powerline Patroller	5
AIR TRANSPORT OPERATING SUPPORT OCCUPATIONS	
Flight Dispatcher	1
Air-Traffic Controller	1
Air-Traffic Control Officer	1
Station Agent	1
Schedule Analyst	1
Traffic Technician	1
Air-Traffic Control Assistant	1

Table 5 continued

Occupational title	Points
MOTOR TRANSPORT OPERATING OCCUPATIONS, not elsewhere classified	
Route Planning Analyst	1
Mobile-Support-Equipment Operator	1
POWER STATION OPERATORS	
Load Dispatcher	1
Substation Inspector	1
Diesel-Plant Operator	1
Power-Switchboard Operator	1
Power-Control-Room Operator	1
Nuclear-Reactor Operator	1
Hydro-Electric-Station Operator	1
Turbine Operator, Steam	1
Field Operator, Nuclear-Generating Station	1
Central Office Power-Room Operator	1
Feeder-Switchboard Operator	1
STATIONARY ENGINE AND AUXILIARY EQUIPMENT OPERATING AND MAINTAINING OCCUPATIONS	
Boiler Operator	5
Refrigeration Operator	5
Diesel Engine Operator, Stationary	5
Power Engineer, General	5
Steam Operator	5
Boiler Operator, Pulverized Coal	5
Building Systems Technician	5
Compressor Operator, Caisson	5
FILM, TELEVISION AND RELATED OCCUPATIONS	
RADIO AND TELEVISION BROADCASTING EQUIPMENT OPERATORS	5
SOUND AND VIDEO RECORDING AND REPRODUCTION EQUIPMENT OPERATORS	
Sound Mixer	5
Stereo-Tape Editor	5

Table 5 continued

Occupational title	Points
Re-Recording Mixer	5
Video-and-Sound-Recorder	5
Video-Recording-Equipment Operator	5
Sound-Effects Technician	5
MOTION PICTURE PROJECTIONISTS	I
PHOTOGRAPHIC PROCESSING OCCUPATIONS	
Photographic Enlarger	I
Negative-Contact-Frame Operator	I
Film Developer	I
Negative Retoucher	I
INSPECTING, TESTING, GRADING AND SAMPLING OCCUPATIONS, not elsewhere classified	
Radiographer, Industrial	3
Tester, Ultrasonic	3

Reprinted by permission of Employment and Immigration Canada.

Those who fail to meet the federal job listings requirements may be granted visas if they're French-speaking and intending to settle in Quebec.

Quebec has a lot of say in who gets immigrant visas to live in that province. And it has its own selection criteria. Because it gives a lot of weight to French language and culture, francophones stand a better chance of getting into Canada if they go to Quebec. In most cases, those approved by Quebec authorities are granted visas, regardless of how they fared under the federal assessment criteria. And of course, once granted permanent resident status, they would be free to live anywhere in Canada.

Table 6
DESIGNATED OCCUPATIONS LIST

Province/Occupational title	Licensing	Target
NEWFOUNDLAND		
Occupational Therapist	Yes	10
Physiotherapist	Yes	10
PRINCE EDWARD ISLAND		
No designations		
NOVA SCOTIA		
No designations		
NEW BRUNSWICK		
Consultations not complete		
QUEBEC		
Exclusive Provincial Selection of Independent Immigrants		
ONTARIO		
Design and Development Engineer	Yes	40
Electronic Engineer, General	Yes	50
Systems Analyst, Business, Electronic Data Processing		50
Systems Analyst, Engineering-Scientific, Electronic Data Processing		30
Systems-Software Programmer		100
Occupational Therapist	Yes	30
Physiotherapist	Yes	40
Radiotherapy Technician (Technologist)	Yes	15
MANITOBA		
No designations		
SASKATCHEWAN		
Psychologist, Clinical	Yes	11
Occupational Therapist	Yes	12
Physiotherapist	Yes	20
ALBERTA		
Consultations not complete		

Table 6 continued

Province/Occupational title	Licensing	Target
BRITISH COLUMBIA		
Electronic Engineer, General	Yes	30
Systems Analyst, Engineering-Scientific		35
Systems-Software Programmer		35
Programmer, Engineering and Scientific		30
Application Programmer		30
Telecommunications Specialist, Computers		20
Speech Pathologist		25
Occupational Therapist	Yes	25
Physiotherapist	Yes	30
Radiotherapy Technician (Technologist)	Yes	10
Dental Hygienist	Yes	30
Head Chef		30
Farmer, Nursery		20
NWT		
No Designations		
YUKON		
No Designations		

Reprinted by permission of Employment and Immigration Canada.

CHAPTER SIX

Business Immigrants

ENTREPRENEURS, INVESTORS AND THE SELF-EMPLOYED

Entrepreneurs, investors, and those self-employed may be considered potential business immigrants. Canada boasts one of the world's most comprehensive business immigration programs. During the application procedure you may be involved with as many as four federal departments or agencies: External Affairs, Employment and Immigration Canada, Investment Canada, and Regional Industrial Expansion.

External Affairs represents Canada abroad through embassies and consular missions. It is there that most business people obtain information about economic conditions in Canada. Visa officers are responsible for counselling and selecting applicants deemed likely to become successfully established in Canada.

Employment and Immigration Canada oversees and carries out policies and programs relating to employment in Canada and selection of immigrants. Once you're admitted to Canada, you will continue to be involved with this section of federal government, not only because of immigration conditions related to your admission to Canada, but also as an employer.

Investment Canada promotes investment in Canadian businesses. Working closely with embassies and consulates abroad, Investment Canada provides investment information and anything else you may want to know about doing business in Canada, both before you leave your country of origin and after you have relocated here.

Regional Industrial Expansion administers most of the programs initiated by the government on behalf of Canada's commercial and industrial sectors. The federal government consists of some 30 additional departments and agencies, but this department most directly represents the business community's individual and collective interests to the federal government.

Both federal and provincial governments actively encourage foreigners to invest in Canada. Indeed, immigration authorities must give priority consideration to applications by prospective business immigrants because of the potential benefit they offer to the Canadian economy. The three basic categories of business immigrant are defined as follows:

1. The category of "entrepreneur" includes experienced business people who wish to buy or start a business in Canada in which they intend to have a managerial role. The business must create jobs for one or more Canadians

and make a significant contribution to Canada's economy. Applicants having managerial experience in small to medium-sized companies are welcome.

2. "Investors" must have a successful business track record and substantial funds to pump into the Canadian economy, namely from $250,000 to $700,000 over a guaranteed period of no less than five years.

3. The "self-employed" are those who intend to establish a business in Canada that will employ only themselves, but will contribute to the economic, cultural or artistic life of Canada. This category includes farmers, sports personalities, artists and owners of small community businesses.

In the point system assessment, entrepreneurs and investors are not assessed on occupation or arranged employment. They are rated only according to those factors which actually affect their ability to become successfully established in Canada. And of course, the arranged employment factor does not apply to the self-employed.

APPLYING FOR A BUSINESS VISA

In all such cases, the first step is to contact the nearest Canadian embassy, consulate or high commission. Applications may then be submitted, and should include the following documents: a resumé including full details relating to the applicant's business, industrial or managerial experience; a financial statement; expected activities in Canada; and intended final destination in Canada.

If necessary, Canadian authorities abroad will assist the applicant in preparing for an exploratory trip to Canada to consider business opportunities in this country.

This may include making appointments with appropriate provincial officials and Canadian business groups or individuals. Such a trip may help the prospective entrepreneur, investor or self-employed immigrant assess conditions in Canada first hand before going ahead with plans for relocating here.

Through the government agency, Investment Canada, prospective investors may obtain information concerning location, financing, planning and systems development, federal and provincial policies regarding taxation, employment, energy and industry regulations. They may also receive help in identifying investment opportunities, locating private-sector professionals and defining investment objectives. The address of Investment Canada is 240 Sparks Street, 5th floor West, P.O. Box 2800, Station D, Ottawa, Ontario, Canada K1P 6A5.

THE INVESTOR PROGRAM

The Immigrant Investor Program was introduced in 1986 to attract to Canada qualified business people who would pump substantial capital into Canadian business ventures. The program is designed to create jobs for Canadians and to generate the necessary funds for smaller businesses to expand. It allows investors to move to this country with their dependents, lock, stock and barrel.

Immigration is a shared federal–provincial responsibility. Indeed, federal regulations give the provinces a key role in assessing the economic impact of foreign investment proposals. (See Table 7 for a list of provincial offices that will assist you.)

Table 7
PROVINCIAL OFFICES GEARED TO
ASSIST INVESTORS

Province	Addresses
Newfoundland	Deputy Minister Department of Career Development and Advanced Studies Beothuck Building Crosbie Place ST JOHN'S, Newfoundland AIC 5T7
Nova Scotia	Senior Project Officer Industrial Promotion Branch Department of Development World Trade and Convention Centre 1800 Argyle Street, Box 519 HALIFAX, Nova Scotia B3J 2R7
New Brunswick	Labour Market Services Branch Department of Labour P.O. Box 6000 FREDERICTON, New Brunswick E3B 5H1
Prince Edward Island	Chief of Research and Planning Prince Edward Island Department of Industry P.O. Box 2000 CHARLOTTETOWN, Prince Edward Island CIA 7N8

Table 7 continued

Province	Addresses
Ontario	Industrial Development Branch Immigrant Entrepreneur Section Ministry of Industry, Trade and Technology 6th Floor, 900 Bay Street Hearst Block, Queen's Park TORONTO, Ontario M7A 2E1
Québec	Chief, Le Service des investisseurs Ministère des Communautés culturelles et de l'Immigration 355, rue McGill MONTRÉAL, Québec H2Y 2E8

Manitoba	*Business applicants:*
	Ministry of Industry, Trade
	  and Technology
	4th Floor, 155 Carlton Street
	WINNIPEG, Manitoba
	R3C 3H8
	
	*Agricultural entrepreneurs and
	  self-employed farmers:*
	Regional Business Immigration
	  Coordinator
	Canada Immigration Centre
	3rd Floor, 2 Lakeview Square
	175 Carlton Street
	WINNIPEG, Manitoba
	R3C 3H9

Table 7 continued

Province	Addresses
Saskatchewan	International Operations Division Economic Development and Trade 3rd Floor, 2103-11th Avenue REGINA, Saskatchewan S4P 3V7
Alberta	Ministry of Career Development and Employment 4th Floor, Park Square 10001 Bellamy Hill EDMONTON, Alberta T5J 3W5
British Columbia	Ministry of Economic Development Suite 315, Robson Square 800 Hornby Street VANCOUVER, British Columbia V6Z 2C5

Reprinted by permission of Employment and Immigration Canada.

Most provinces have specific guidelines that have to be met before a proposal may be favourably considered by Immigration. Federal visa officers located in Canadian consulates abroad are responsible for processing investors's applications.

Investors may choose to come to Canada under one of three tiers of investment:

I. A personal net worth of at least $500,000 and an investment of $250,000 locked in for five years in a province which, in the previous year, received fewer than 10 per cent of all business immigrants.

2. A personal net worth of at least $500,000 and $350,000 locked in for five years in a province which, in the previous year, received 10 per cent or more of all business immigrants.

3. A personal net worth of $700,000 or more and a commitment of an investment of $500,000 for a five-year period, in any part of Canada.

Quebec has adopted its own regulations for investors, even though they must be consistent with federal objectives. Quebec's investor program is administered separately from federal guidelines so those considering an investment in Quebec should consult Quebec's immigration service.

Once your application as an investor is approved and you're given your visa, you may enter Canada as a permanent resident.

Conditional Landing

If you have excellent business experience but no firm business proposal for a Canadian venture, you may be granted a conditional visa. It would allow you to move to Canada with your family dependents, and would give you two years to develop a business venture that would gain provincial support and create jobs for Canadians. Although you are admitted to Canada as a permanent resident, such landed immigrant status remains conditional and if, after two years, you have not fulfilled the conditions of your coming to Canada, you may be required to leave the country.

CHAPTER SEVEN

The Canada–United States Free Trade Agreement (FTA) and the North American Free Trade Agreement (NAFTA)

The Free Trade Agreement with the United States has made it easier for Canadians and Americans to work temporarily in each other's country. The agreement covers business visitors, traders and investors, professionals and intra-company transfers. It applies only to citizens of Canada and the United States.

The agreement allows certain business people to come

to Canada without having to obtain work permits. These people are processed by immigration officers at port of entry. These include those in research and design, growth, manufacture and production, harvester owners, purchasing and production personnel, marketing researchers, trade fair and promotional personnel, sales representatives (taking orders only), after-sales specialized service personnel for repair, installation, or maintenance requirements for warranty obligations, general-service professionals paid by the source country, management personnel, computer specialists, financial services personnel, public relations and advertising personnel, tourism personnel, translators and interpreters. (See Table 8.)

The North American Free Trade Agreement will substantially boost Canada's exports to Mexican markets. Within NAFTA, Canada and Mexico have a separate agreement on agricultural trade. Mexico's market will be opened through the immediate elimination of import licences and the phase-out of tariffs.

The agreement with Mexico also allows full access to Mexico's financial institutions, after a transition period. Canadian banks, trust companies, securities brokers and insurance companies will be able to open subsidiaries, invest in, and acquire ownership of financial institutions in Mexico.

Immigration regulations are to be gradually amended to allow easy movement of business personnel and professionals between Canada and Mexico, similar to the immigration provisions in the agreement with the United States. However, at the time of going to press, these changes had yet to be fully spelled out. Some phases of the agreement with Mexico will not come into force until 1994 and after.

Table 8
QUALIFYING PROFESSIONS AND CAREERS
UNDER THE FREE TRADE AGREEMENT

Profession	Qualification
Accountant	• baccalaureate degree
Architect	• baccalaureate degree or state/provincial licence
Computer systems analyst	• baccalaureate degree
Disaster relief claims adjuster	• a claims adjuster employed by an insurance company located in the United States or an independent claims adjuster who has successfully completed training in the appropriate areas of insurance adjustment pertaining to disaster relief claims and who has at least three years of experience in claims adjustment or a baccalaureate degree. NOTE: For the purposes of this profession, a disaster shall be an event so declared by the Insurance Bureau of Canada or a sub-committee thereof through activating the Insurance Emergency Response Plan.
Economist	• baccalaureate degree
Engineer	• baccalaureate degree or state/provincial licence
Forester	• baccalaureate degree or state/provincial licence
Graphic designer	• baccalaureate degree, or post-secondary diploma and three years' experience

Table 8 continued

Profession	Qualification
Hotel manager	• baccalaureate degree and three years' experience NOTE: This refers to the management position to which other managers report, e.g., general manager, director.
Land surveyor	• baccalaureate degree or state/provincial/federal licence
Landscape architect	• baccalaureate degree
Lawyer	• L.L.B., J.D., L.L.L., B.C.L., or membership in a state/provincial bar
Librarian	• M.L.S., or B.L.S. (for which another baccalaureate degree was a prerequisite)
Management consultant	• baccalaureate degree or equivalent professional experience as established by statement or professional credential attesting to five years' experience as a management consultant, or five years' experience in a field of specialty related to the consulting agreement NOTES: 1. A management consultant provides services which are directed toward improving the managerial, operating, and economic performance of public and private entities by analyzing and resolving strategic and operating problems. Thus, the entity's goals, objectives, policies, strategies, administration, organization, and operation are improved.

Table 8 continued

Profession	Qualification
	2. A management consultant is an independent contractor or an employee of a consulting firm under contract to a Canadian entity.
	3. A management consultant can be a salaried employee of a Canadian entity to which services are being provided only when an existing position or a newly-created position is not being occupied. As a salaried employee of such a Canadian entity, only a supernumerary temporary position may be occupied.
	4. A management consultant can be coming to occupy a permanent position on a temporary basis with a Canadian management consulting firm.
Mathematician	• baccalaureate degree
Medical/allied professional	
Clinical lab technologist	• baccalaureate degree
Dentist	• D.D.S., D.M.D., or state/provincial licence
Dietician	• baccalaureate degree or state/provincial licence
Medical technologist	• baccalaureate degree
Nutritionist	• baccalaureate degree

Table 8 continued

Profession	Qualification
Occupational therapist	• baccalaureate degree or state/provincial licence
Pharmacist	• baccalaureate degree or state/provincial licence
Physician (teaching and/ or research only)	• M.D. or state/provincial licence
Physio/physical therapist	• baccalaureate degree or state/provincial licence
Psychologist	• state/provincial licence
Recreational therapist	• baccalaureate degree
Registered nurse	• state/provincial licence
Veterinarian	• D.V.M., D.M.V., or state/provincial licence
Range manager (range conser- vationist)	• baccalaureate degree
Research assistant (working in a post-secondary educational institution)	• baccalaureate degree
Scientific technician/ technologist:	• Must A. work in direct support of professionals in the following disciplines: chemistry, geology, geophysics, meteorology,

Table 8 continued

Profession	Qualification
	physics, astronomy, agricultural sciences, biology, or forestry; B. possess theoretical knowledge of the discipline; C. solve practical problems in the discipline; and D. apply principles of the discipline to basic or applied research.
Scientist	• a baccalaureate degree is the minimum educational requirement for all professions in this category: • *agriculturalist (agronomist)* • *geneticist* • *animal breeder* • *geologist* • *animal scientist* • *geophysicist* • *apiculturist* • *horticulturist* • *astronomer* • *meteorologist* • *biologist* • *pharmacologist* • *biochemist* • *physicist* • *chemist* • *plant breeder* • *dairy scientist* • *poultry scientist* • *entomologist* • *soil scientist* • *epidemiologist* • *zoologist*
Social worker	• baccalaureate degree
Sylviculturist (forestry specialist)	• baccalaureate degree
Teacher *college*	• baccalaureate degree
seminary	• baccalaureate degree

Table 8 continued

Profession	Qualification
Teacher *university*	• baccalaureate degree
Technical publications writer	• baccalaureate degree, or post-secondary diploma and three years' experience
Urban planner	• baccalaureate degree
Vocational counselor	• baccalaureate degree The terms "state/provincial licence" and "state/provincial/federal licence" mean any document issued by a state, provincial, or federal government as the case may be, or under its authority, which permits a person to engage in a regulated activity or profession.

Reprinted by permission of Employment and Immigration Canada.

CHAPTER EIGHT

Other Visas

EMPLOYMENT VISAS

Only permanent residents and citizens have the right to work in Canada. All others must obtain authorization in the form of "work permits". Most work permits (visas) must be obtained outside Canada, except in special cases, such as refugee claimants and those approved in principle for landing from within Canada.

Work permits are frequently issued to seasonal workers, such as farm workers, and to those recruited abroad for skilled jobs for which Canadian workers are not readily available. They are also granted to foreign nannies and other household workers who come to Canada under the Live-in Caregiver Program. Such employment must meet certain working standards and conditions and must be approved by a Canada Employment Centre.

THE LIVE-IN CAREGIVER PROGRAM

This program, introduced in 1992, replaced the former Foreign Domestic Movement Program, which since 1981 had permitted thousands of domestics and nannies to work in Canada, with the promise of an opportunity to gain permanent resident status. The new program allows qualified foreign workers to take jobs in Canada as nannies or caretakers for the elderly and the disabled. After two years in Canada they may be considered for permanent resident status. The former Domestics' program was not as demanding as to workers' education and training.

Caregivers are granted work visas on the basis of their qualifications, experience and personal suitability. They must have a working knowledge of English or French and possess the equivalent of a Grade 12 education and at least six months' full-time training in care-related service. Indeed, the applicant's work skills must be directly linked to the job requirements in Canada. Household chores may be combined with caregiving duties. However, visa approval hinges on the element of caregiving required by a prospective employer.

The application procedure is as follows: to obtain a visa as a live-in caregiver your employer must first submit a request to hire you at a Canada Employment Centre. Provided there are no Canadian residents or other temporary workers in Canada able and willing to take the job, the employment offer is then channelled to the visa office in your country. You will then be asked to attend an interview in which to prove your skills. If you are approved, and if you pass the medical examination, you will be given the go-ahead to work in Canada.

Live-in caregivers are protected by the same employment conditions enjoyed by all Canadians. Employment standards cover rights in areas including vacation time with pay; overtime pay; paid public holidays; minimum wage and other benefits such as pregnancy leave and notice of termination of employment.

If you're not happy with your employer you may work for someone else. Regardless of what your employer may tell you, immigration authorities will not deport you for leaving him or her. However, you must notify Immigration in advance of doing so. You must also obtain a fresh employment visa before you can go to another employer. After two years, you will be given an opportunity to apply for permanent residence — a process that may take as long as two years to complete. However, once "approval in principle" is obtained, you will be given an "open" work permit.

This permit allows you to switch to office work, factory jobs or whatever employment you are offered. But until you gain permanent resident status, you must obtain Immigration's permission before you go to another employer. The requirement of two years' employment does not include any time spent outside of Canada. If you take a holiday abroad for three summer months, for example, that time will not be considered part of the two-year period. It is also important to remember that nationals of certain countries must have valid visitor visas to return to Canada. You may need to reapply for a visa in order to resume your job as a caregiver.

The Live-In Caregiver Program is not intended to allow those who fail to obtain visas in other work skills to come to Canada as caregivers. But if you are denied an immigrant visa on the basis of your regular work skills, you are not barred from coming to Canada as a caregiver, provided you have the necessary skills and experience. It is the only program that offers temporary foreign workers the opportunity to become permanent residents. It is often a good way to gain entry to Canada. For example, through the former Foreign Domestic Movement Program, many young women who were pharmacists, engineers, nurses and teachers, in their countries of origin, gained permanent resident status in Canada after first becoming domestics and working as household helpers here.

STUDENT VISAS

Foreign students wishing to study in Canada must obtain authorization from a visa office prior to coming to Canada. To acquire a visa you must produce a valid passport, a letter from the school confirming acceptance and a list of the courses to be studied. You will also be required to show that you have sufficient money for all tuition fees and living expenses during the study period.

Dependents may be permitted to join students in Canada, but, in most cases they are not allowed to work. Exceptions are made, however, for humanitarian reasons, as in the case of a cut-off of funds from the country of origin because of politics or other unforeseen circumstances.

Unless the school provides health care insurance, it is highly recommended that you purchase adequate private insurance. School officials will counsel you in such matters.

The cost of living in Canada varies from province to province. The visa office will tell you what expenses you can expect in the part of Canada you will be staying in. Generally speaking, the most expensive province in which to live is Ontario. There you will be expected to have sufficient funds to cover expenses of about $8,000 a year, if single, and about $15,000, if accompanied by a dependent. The income level requirement is increased by $1,000 for each additional dependent. By comparison, if you go to Quebec, you would need about 20 per cent less funding.

Foreign students may be granted work permits while attending school in Canada, although certain restrictions do apply. Usually, one of the following conditions must be applicable:

• The student may want to work as a graduate assistant.

• Funding from home may have been interrupted because of political or other difficulties in his or her country.

• The employment may be an integral part of the student's studies, such as a work term in a co-op program.

• The employment may be on campus.

• The student may want to work in a study-related employment following graduation. In this case, a work permit is granted for up to one year.

Visa students who work without Immigration's permission risk being ordered to leave Canada before their school term is finished. Foreign students are strongly advised to alert immigration authorities if there are any unforeseen changes to their study programs, funding, or other circumstances.

For more information on educational opportunities and conditions, write to one of the following organizations:

Degree Studies:

Canadian Bureau for International Education, 85 Albert Street, Suite 1400, Ottawa, Ontario, Canada K1P 6A4.

Association of Universities and Colleges of Canada, 151 Slater Street, Ottawa, Ontario Canada K1P 5N1.

Technical and other non-degree courses:

Association of Canadian Community Colleges, 110 Eglinton Avenue West, 2nd floor, Toronto, Ontario, Canada M4R 1A3.

Private Institutions:

Association of Canadian Career Colleges, 40 Charing Cross, Box 340, Brantford, Ontario, Canada N3T 5N3.

A reminder: Quebec has its own immigration services, operating in conjunction with federal immigration authorities. Foreign students wishing to attend Quebec schools must obtain separate approval from Quebec immigration officials. Information about foreign student admissions to schools in Quebec may be obtained by writing to Ministère des Communautés culturelles et de l'Immigration du Québec, Direction des étudiants, 355, rue Ste-Catherine ouest (5e étage) Montréal, Québec, Canada H3B 1A4.

CHAPTER NINE

Exemption from Outside Application

The Immigration Act requires that those who seek permanent residence in Canada apply for visas from outside Canada. In some cases, however, such a requirement creates undue hardship. For this reason, applications for permanent residence from within Canada may be permitted when special consideration is deemed justified.

THE SUPREME COURT RULING

The Supreme Court of Canada has ruled that immigration officers are obligated to consider requests for an exemption from immigration regulations for public policy reasons or on compassionate and humanitarian grounds.

The court has also ruled that immigration officers, in the name of the minister, must deal with such requests and advise the petitioners of the result. Immigration officers may thereby decide that a case warrants special consideration for an exemption on humanitarian and compassionate grounds, or for reasons of public policy, or that special relief is not warranted in such a case.

Because of this court decision, immigration officers are advised to use their "good judgment" in dealing with inland applications for permanent resident status, and they are reminded that such consideration not only benefits applicants, but also reflects "the objectives of the Immigration Act in upholding Canada's humanitarian traditions."

The overall review process demands a case-by-case response; officers are expected to consider carefully all aspects of the situation, and to use their best judgment to make an "informed" recommendation.

HUMANITARIAN AND COMPASSIONATE GROUNDS

"Humanitarian and compassionate grounds" exist when unusual, undeserved or disproportionate hardship would result in forcing the applicant to leave Canada only to be processed for an immigrant visa allowing him or her to return to Canada — for example, a visiting elderly mother whose children want her to remain in Canada with them. Other than medical and security screenings, sponsorship is routinely approved. It would be an "unreasonable hardship" to force her to return to her country of origin to await sponsorship, as this might involve a separation of two years or more before she could be with her children again.

PUBLIC POLICY SITUATIONS

"Public policy" applies to those situations that warrant consideration from within Canada because of the immigration program, not necessarily because humanitarian grounds exist.

For example, requests for visa exemption made by spouses of Canadian residents may be "sympathetically examined," when separation of spouses entails hardship which warrants the exercise of special relief. In practice, when a marriage is considered to be of "substance and of likely duration," entered into in good faith, and not a marriage of convenience, for immigration sponsorship purposes, approval is often given.

Illegal *de facto* Residents: such illegal aliens are defined as "persons illegally in Canada and unknown to immigration authorities." These persons, until they identify themselves, have never been "reported" by an immigration officer, have never made a refugee claim, or they have skipped an immigration inquiry and have remained here illegally. In other words, immigration authorities had no idea they were in Canada. They have established roots in Canada. They may have purchased homes and may have raised and educated children in Canada; their children may be Canadian citizens by birth. So, although they have no legal status in Canada, they have lived here so long and are so established that, in fact if not in law, they have their residence in Canada and not abroad. Such persons have severed their ties with their home country, and would face undue hardship if required to leave Canada in order to seek a visa to return legally as permanent residents.

Applications for permanent residence may be considered sympathetically in the case of long-term holders of work permits. The guidelines in such cases are to be considered similar to guidelines governing *de facto* residents. The principal criterion will be the applicant's long-term prospects for continuation of his or her employment in Canada and integration in Canadian society.

There may be other situations deemed to warrant the granting of landed status from within Canada. These would involve conditions having a considerable impact on the economic, cultural, social or scientific aspects of Canadian society.

Although family reunification is a stated objective of immigration policy, there are cases when the regulations do not always reflect this. The law provides for the acceptance of certain applicants who do not satisfy normal conditions, but nonetheless should be permitted to live in Canada on humanitarian and compassionate grounds. Immigration officers are advised to keep in mind that some cases may warrant special consideration because of the financial or emotional needs of the Canadian sponsor.

Who qualifies for special consideration?

• An individual who is not a family member by blood may have a long-term relationship warranting special consideration on humanitarian or compassionate grounds. For example, a child raised by a grandmother, or a child adopted by relatives through non-legal channels may qualify for special consideration by immigration authorities. In such a case, the child would be a *de facto* family member.

• An elderly, unmarried or widowed relative, who has lived in the home of a married niece for a long time, may be considered a family dependent on compassionate grounds because she would have no one else to turn to for support.

• A last remaining single brother or sister whose parents are both dead and who is dependent on a sibling residing in Canada may qualify.

• An unmarried or widowed family member who, while not dependent on the migrating family at the time he or she left for Canada, has subsequently clearly re-established dependency on the family in Canada, such as in the case of serious injury, or if a family loses the primary wage earner.

• An aged, unmarried or widowed servant who resides with or previously resided with the Canadian resident family prior to the family's departure for Canada may qualify.

CHAPTER TEN

Immigration Control

VISITORS

The Immigration Act defines a "visitor" to Canada as "a person who is lawfully admitted to Canada, or seeks to enter Canada, for a temporary purpose."

Visitors are allowed to enter Canada as a privilege, not a right. Those wishing to work or study in Canada must normally obtain authorization from visa offices abroad prior to coming to Canada. In most cases, visitors may not change their status. A person admitted as a tourist may not become a student; a temporary worker cannot change jobs; and a student may not change schools.

Visas may be required of others who simply wish to holiday in Canada. Indeed, Canada has imposed visitor visa requirements on more than 100 countries (See

Appendix 2). It is the responsibility of potential visitors to make sure they know how visa requirements may affect them. Possession of a visitor visa, work permit, or other travel document does not necessarily guarantee your admission to Canada. The examining officer at the airport or other port of entry must be satisfied that such documents are valid, and that circumstances have not changed since the visa or work permit was issued.

Visitors are admitted to Canada for six months, unless otherwise specified. If they remain in Canada longer than permitted, or otherwise break immigration law or regulations, such as by unlawfully accepting employment or attending a school without authorization, they automatically become "illegally in Canada" and subject to removal.

PORTS OF ENTRY; POSTING OF BONDS; CANADA CUSTOMS

All those seeking admission to Canada — whether visitors, immigrants or permanent residents returning to Canada after an extended stay abroad — are questioned by an immigration officer on arrival in Canada. The immigration officer must be satisfied that the person is either a genuine visitor or a former resident who has not lost his or her resident status in Canada. Those whose admission is rejected are required to go before an adjudicator at an immigration inquiry. Those who do not wish to go to the inquiry may be permitted to leave Canada.

In some cases, a visitor may be required to post a bond to guarantee that the terms of admission will be met. The deposit, which may be in the form of a promissory note given by a relative in Canada, is cancelled when the visitor leaves Canada.

Immigrants may bring to Canada duty-free all of their personal belongings including cars, jewellery and other luxury items they have owned and have had in their possession before coming to Canada. Normally, this means the goods are used items and have been in the immigrant's possession for a period of six months or more. The only exception applies to gifts received by a bride just prior to coming to this country.

PERMANENT RESIDENT CARD

Permanent residents who are not Canadian citizens may lose their right to remain in Canada upon conviction of a serious crime. They also risk forfeiting resident status by remaining abroad too long.

Permanent residents who go outside Canada for more than 183 days in any 12-month period are presumed to have abandoned Canada, unless they satisfy immigration authorities that they never intended to give up Canadian residence. Until recently, those going abroad for an extended period were advised to apply for a Returning Resident Permit, which was valid for one year.

This permit is no longer issued. Now, immigrants are issued a Permanent Resident Card, which is good for three years, by which time they would have the required residence to apply for Canadian citizenship. In any case, the card, a plastic, machine-readable, wallet-size document, should not be allowed to expire until the bearer becomes a Canadian citizen. While possession of such a document is not mandatory, it is generally accepted as proof that the bearer continues to consider Canada his or her home. If you were to go abroad for more than six months with an expired Permanent Resident Card, you would be assumed to have abandoned Canadian residence. The onus would be on you to prove you hadn't.

Not all immigrants who establish permanent residence in another country forfeit Canadian residence. Children often do not. For example, an immigrant child taken away from Canada by parents who decide to abandon Canadian residence is "not deemed to have abandoned Canadian residence," if he or she returns to Canada as soon as possible when grown. In other words, such children are considered to have retained Canadian resident status if they can satisfy immigration authorities they have continued to think of Canada as their home when living abroad, and always had the intention of moving back to Canada as soon as they were old enough to do so.

Many former Canadian residents have forfeited their right to return to this country because they embraced the citizenship of another country. Indeed, many Canadians who took American citizenship prior to February 15, 1977, have been shocked to discover that although born and raised in Canada, they're "foreigners" in the eyes of Canadian immigration officials, and are required to qualify for immigrant visas to live in Canada again. That is because prior to the 1977 change in Canadian citizenship law, Canadian citizenship was automatically lost in taking the citizenship of another country. Now, with the new Citizenship Act, Canada recognizes dual and multiple citizenships.

In recognition of former citizens' ties with Canada, Ottawa has for some time been considering changes in the law to make it easier for former Canadians to regain citizenship. A likely option is to remove the present requirement that former citizens must first immigrate to Canada. Until then, immigration officers are directed to "sympathetically consider" applications by former Canadian citizens.

EXCLUDED CLASSES

The Immigration Act bars entry to people who may pose a threat to public health, safety, order, or national security. Also inadmissible are those not having a visible means of support or proper travel documents.

Inadmissibility for health reasons is based on risk to public health or safety, or excessive demands on health or social services. Inadmissibility on criminal grounds is determined by the sentence under which the visitor would be liable according to Canadian law. Admission may be granted following rehabilitation. The law also provides for the exclusion or removal of those believed to be linked to organized crime or terrorist groups. Canadian statutes classify offences as being punishable by indictment, by summary conviction, or by either, at the option of the prosecution.

Indictible crimes include murder, manslaughter, robbery, sexual assault, theft over a certain amount, drug trafficking, forgery and kidnapping. Summary offences are less serious and may include drunk driving, possession of a narcotic, prostitution or common assault.

For immigration purposes, those convicted of an indictible offence are deemed inadmissible. Those convicted of two or more summary convictions are also considered inadmissible; however, the bar is lifted when only one conviction or sentence is being served, or has yet to be served within the five years prior to the application, two years in the case those under 21.

A person convicted after having been tried by way of summary conviction of an offence which, at the discretion of the court, could have been tried by way of indictment, is considered guilty only of a crime punishable by way of summary conviction.

However, the choice of trial procedures followed by the courts abroad is irrelevant. Any conviction abroad for a crime that in a Canadian court would be liable either as a summary *or* indictible offence, would be considered indictible by Immigration.

Thus, while, for example, in Canada petty theft may be tried by way of either summary or indictible conviction, it is generally tried by way of summary conviction. However, such a conviction abroad, regardless of the lightness of the sentence, would be considered as a conviction tried by way of indictment, for Canadian immigration purposes.

Where a person has been convicted of one or more offences which (a) would make him a juvenile offender in Canada or (b) would not be punishable under Canadian law, or (c) occurred only once and in Canada would be punishable by summary conviction only, such a person is not to be considered inadmissible on criminal grounds.

DEPORTATION

Immigration law provides for the forced deportation of a person expelled from Canada. A deportation means a permanent bar from this country. Re-entry may be gained only with the consent of the Minister of Immigration.

The law, however, also provides for the removal of foreigners under less severe measures. A person who has committed a minor offence, or has not complied with immigration regulations on arrival — such as not having proper identification or travel documents — may be permitted to leave the country under a "voluntary withdrawal."

Otherwise, an "exclusion order" may be issued by which a person is barred from re-entering Canada for one year. If a visitor already admitted to Canada has committed a minor infraction of immigration law, a "departure order" may be issued rather than the much more severe "deportation order." In such a case, once the person has left Canada, the order is no longer in force and the person may apply to re-enter Canada any time.

MINISTER'S PERMIT

A Minister's Permit may be issued to people normally deemed inadmissible to this country. It also allows those ordered to leave Canada to remain here. Permits may be issued to allow such inadmissible people to enter Canada temporarily for funerals and other mercy visits. Often, they are issued to allow people with medical problems to be reunited with loved ones in Canada; to permit those here illegally to apply for permanent resident status; or to allow refugee claimants and others who come to Canada with no valid travel documents to remain here. Indeed, Minister's Permits allow the bearer to go abroad and return without the need to obtain fresh visitor visas, or otherwise obtain clearance by immigration authorities. Minister's Permit holders do not require Immigration's permission to go to school in Canada.

Persons to whom Minister's Permits have been issued are not considered visitors or immigrants. They are in a separate category and known simply as "permit holders."

Minister's Permits are required when it is established that the family reunification, refugee settlement or national interest factors are sufficiently strong to justify special authorization to allow the holders to enter or remain in Canada when otherwise denied admission here because of a medical condition or a criminal record.

CHAPTER ELEVEN

Application
Information

PRE-APPLICATION QUESTIONNAIRES

Until recently, most visa offices required prospective immigrants to fill out a "pre-application questionnaire" before the regular application form could be submitted and fees paid.

Indeed, many prospective immigrants were denied an opportunity to make a formal application, on the basis that pre-screening indicated that the applicant would not qualify for a visa.

But the courts have ruled that nobody may be denied an application form, and now all prospective immigrants are routinely invited to submit formal applications, along with the prescribed application fees.

IMMIGRATION FEES

On February 3, 1986, the Canada Employment and Immigration Commission began charging fees for certain immigration services. The cost recovery program was designed to help offset the cost of immigration operations. Since then, fees have increased substantially. (See Table 9 for the immigration fee schedule.)

For permanent residence applications, the fee must be paid at the time of the application. If a relative in Canada submits a sponsorship application, he or she must pay the fee. Convention Refugees and those who enter Canada under any government humanitarian program are normally exempt from such fees.

All fees must be paid in Canadian dollars in Canada and/or the equivalent local currency overseas. Fees apply whether a visa application is approved or not. There are no refunds.

A visitor visa fee exemption applies for persons who come from countries on which Canada has imposed visitor visa requirements, or those travelling in Canada for less than 48 hours, provided they are part of an organized tour operated by a transportation company which originates and returns to the United States.

Table 9
IMMIGRATION FEES

Type	Cost
Application for permanent residence:	
Applicant plus one dependent	$450
Dependent under age 19 who is not a spouse	$50
Dependent 19 and over or spouse	$450
Entrepreneur, investor, self-employed:	
Applicant plus one dependent	$750
Dependent under 19, who is not a spouse	$50
Dependent 19 and over or spouse	$450
Family Business Application	$250
Certificate of Record of Landing:	
Individual	$25
Family	$50
Visitor Visa:	
Individual	$50
Family	$100
Collective Certificate (per person)	$40
Visitor Visa Extension:	
Individual	$50
Family	$100
Discretionary Entry:	
Individual	$75
Family	$150
Group (2 to 14) of entertainers	$150
Student Authorization:	
Individual	$75
Family	$150
Employment Authorization:	
Individual	$100
Family	$200
Group (2 to 14) of entertainers	$200

Table 9 continued

Type	Cost
Replacement of Immigration Record:	
Individual	$25
Family	$50
Combination of Documents, Maximum Rate	$225
Minister's Permit:	
Individual	$100
Family	$200
Group (2 to 14) of entertainers	$200
Extension to Minister's Permit:	
Individual	$100
Family	$200
Group (2 to 14) of entertainers	$200
Minister's Consent to return after Deportation:	
Individual	$250
Criminal Rehabilitation:	
Individual	$250
Transcript of Inquiry:	
Each transcript	$75
Investment Proposal Assessment:	
Each proposal	$4,500
Investment Proposal Amendment:	
Each proposal	$1,500
File Transfer:	
Each Request	$50
(Fees in effect at the time of going to press.)	

Reprinted by permission of Employment and Immigration Canada.

PART TWO

Citizenship

CHAPTER TWELVE

Canadian Citizenship

WHO IS A CANADIAN CITIZEN?

A Canadian citizen is a person who acquired the citizenship of this country either by birth, or through the legal process of naturalization. This applies to:

- All those born in Canada, except those born to non-residents when one or both parents are foreign diplomats or consular officers, or other representatives or employees in Canada of a foreign government.

- Those born abroad of at least one Canadian citizen parent.

- Domiciled British subjects who gained citizenship automatically on January 1, 1947 when Canada's first Citizenship Act came into force.

- Foreign women who married Canadians and who moved to Canada prior to January 1, 1947. Such women are often called "war brides" for citizenship purposes.

- Immigrants who are granted citizenship by naturalization after having met residence, security and other requirements.

- People for whom normal requirements are waived by the Governor-in-Council (federal cabinet), in order to alleviate cases of special and unusual hardship, or to reward services of an exceptional value to Canada.

The term "domiciled" had a particular meaning under Canada's first Citizenship Act. It applied to legally admitted immigrants who were residents of Canada for five years or more. A British subject automatically had a claim to citizenship if he or she had established Canadian domicile status or, regardless of how he or she came to this country, if he or she had lived in Canada for at least 20 years immediately preceding January 1, 1947.

Unusual circumstances of citizenship would include a person deemed to be born in Canada if born on a Canadian ship as defined in the Canada Shipping Act, on an air cushion vehicle registered in Canada, or on an aircraft registered in Canada.

Similarly, a child found deserted in Canada and considered to be under seven years old is deemed Canadian born — unless the contrary becomes evident within seven years after the child is found.

So too, a minor — a person under the age of 18 — may be granted citizenship any time after admission to Canada if one parent is a Canadian citizen, or at least one parent is embracing Canadian citizenship. Those 14 and older must sign the application, and take and sign the Oath of Canadian Citizenship.

A child born abroad who is adopted by Canadians may be granted Canadian citizenship only after legal admission to Canada. Adoption does not bestow citizenship.

War brides and automatic citizenship

During World War II, large numbers of Canadian army, navy and airforce men married British or European women. Those brides who were not British automatically gained "British subject" status by marriage. Those who had moved to Canada by January 1, 1947, when the country's first Citizenship Act came into force, automatically gained citizenship. They were exempted from the five-year residence (domicile) that was then required of other British subjects in order to gain Canadian citizenship automatically.

The documents and procedures necessary for a war bride to obtain proof of Canadian citizenship are as follows:

• The husband's proof of Canadian citizenship (generally his birth certificate will do).
• Proof of marriage to a Canadian citizen.
• The war bride's own birth certificate.
• Proof of legal admission to Canada. This may be the original document or a copy of the immigration record, available from any Canada Immigration Centre.

First, complete the application for proof of citizenship and then submit the required documents and the prescribed fee in person to any office of the court of Canadian citizenship. Bring two photographs of yourself 35 mm x 43 mm (1.4 in. x 1.7 in.), with an additional 10 mm (0.4 in.) strip at the bottom for your signature, which you must sign in front of a citizenship officer at the time you submit the application at the citizenship office.

After examining the documents, the citizenship officer will confirm your signature and witness your declaration. The certificate will be mailed to your home address.

CHILDREN BORN ABROAD

Under Canada's first Citizenship Act, children born abroad had a claim to Canadian citizenship only if the father was a Canadian citizen; having a Canadian mother and a foreign father did not entitle a child to Canadian citizenship, unless the child was born out of wedlock. This law also required that children born abroad be registered with Canadian consulates. And, in order to retain Canadian citizenship, they had to formally declare, between the ages of 20 and 24, their wish to remain Canadian. Otherwise, they had to be living in Canada on their twenty-fourth birthday. Those who failed to comply with these retention conditions forfeited Canadian citizenship.

This first act was amended, however, on February 15, 1977, and the new act removed discrimination between the sexes by bestowing citizenship on children born abroad when either birth parent was a Canadian citizen. It also revoked retention conditions. Those born abroad no longer had to be registered.

DUAL AND MULTIPLE CITIZENSHIP

Unlike Canada's first Citizenship Act, the present act recognizes dual and multiple citizenships. For example, a British-born Canadian citizen who moves to the U.S. and embraces U.S. citizenship would be considered a citizen of all three countries, and would be entitled to hold passports of all three.

But when the law was changed in 1977 to permit dual and multiple citizenship, those who had previously forfeited Canadian citizenship by embracing the citizenship of another country did not regain it. However, the federal government does recognize the ties that bind former Canadian citizens to this country, and immigration authorities are directed to "consider sympathetically" applications by former Canadians who wish to return to this country.

The amended legislation also allows those who were born abroad, but who were never registered, to file a "delayed registration." And, as explained above, those born abroad to a Canadian mother and a foreign father, previously denied Canadian citizenship, now have the right to be granted citizenship. Such children have the right to apply for Canadian citizenship through Canadian consulates abroad.

As already mentioned, children born in Canada

have no claim to Canadian citizenship if at the time of their birth:

• Neither parent was a Canadian citizen or permanent resident, and one or both parents was a diplomatic or consular officer, or other representative or employee in Canada of a foreign government.

• Or if one of such non-resident parents was an employee in the service of such personnel, an officer or employee in Canada of a specialized agency of the United Nations, or an officer or employee in Canada of any international organization granted diplomatic privileges and immunities.

A child born after the death of either parent is considered to have been born before the death of that parent. Hence, a child born abroad to a single Canadian citizen is considered a Canadian, although the Canadian parent may be dead by the time the child is born. A child born in Canada to non-resident parents, including at least one parent who is in Canada on foreign government service, would be denied Canadian citizenship, although the parent in the foreign service dies before the child is born.

THE RESIDENCE REQUIREMENT

The 1977 Citizenship Act did not simply modify the former statute, it repealed it. In the process, citizenship evolved from a privilege to a right. A landed immigrant who satisfies the stipulated conditions must be granted citizenship.

The present citizenship act requires that an applicant accumulate three years of residence in Canada during the four years immediately preceding the application. But the act does not define "residence," "resident" or "having resided." Whether or not the applicant fulfils the residency requirement is the decision of the citizenship judge. This is because legal admission confers only status. The notion of residence is a completely different concept which considers integration into the community.

If either the applicant or the citizenship minister wants to appeal the citizenship judge's decision, the case may go before the Federal Court of Canada, Trial Division. Decisions by the courts over the past several years suggest weight is given to the fact that although the applicant may not have been "physically present" in Canada for the entire three-year period, he or she continued to consider Canada the principal place of abode.

The following are some court findings in dealing with citizenship residence:

The words "residence" and "resident" of the new Citizenship Act are not as strictly limited to actual presence in Canada throughout the periods as they were in the former statute, but can include, as well, situations in which the person concerned has a place in Canada which is used by him during the period as a place of abode to a sufficient extent to demonstrate the reality of his residing there during the material period, even though he is away from it part of the time.

A person with an established home of his own in which he lives does not cease to be a resident there when he leaves it for a temporary purpose whether on business or vacation or even to pursue a course of study. The fact of his family remaining there while he is away may lend support for the conclusion that he has not ceased to reside there. That conclusion must be reached, as well, even though the absence may be more or less lengthy. It is also enhanced if he returns there frequently when the opportunity to do so arises.

Each case is determined on its own merits and a multitude of factors are considered: the reason for going abroad, whether for business, holiday or studies; the temporary nature of the absence; whether family members stayed behind in Canada; and whether the applicant has returned to Canada whenever it was reasonable to do so.

Indeed, the courts have made it quite clear that while a long absence occasioned by circumstances beyond your control may not have adverse effects on your citizenship application, on the other hand, residence cannot be established "by mere visits to, or temporary stays" in Canada. You must be able to present evidence which suggests a certain integration into Canadian society in terms of work, home and other ties, upon which a judge may base his or her assessment that you have become a part of Canadian society.

RENUNCIATION AND LOSS OF CITIZENSHIP

In general, citizenship is for life. However, one may be stripped of Canadian citizenship if it is obtained fraudulently and, under certain conditions, citizenship may be renounced.

If renunciation is necessary in order to acquire another nationality — as in the case of a foreign-born Canadian who abandons Canadian residence and wants to regain his or her former citizenship — a formal application for renunciation will be considered. The person must be over 18 and living abroad. Taking an oath which contains a declaration of renunciation of Canadian citizenship will not in itself cause loss of citizenship. However, a loss of citizenship may occur in the second generation of Canadians born abroad after February 14, 1977, unless steps are taken to affirm Canadian citizenship through a Canadian consulate abroad, or unless residence, business or other close ties with Canada have been established for at least one year before the individual turns 28.

For some time prior to Canada's first Citizenship Act, female British subjects married to non-British men automatically ceased to be British, and, on January 1, 1947, when the first Act automatically bestowed citizenship on British subjects born in Canada, those same women did not become Canadian citizens.

Canada's first Citizenship Act, however, recognized this unfair penalty and made a provision to rectify it. The act stated that such women, who would otherwise be Canadians, may readily claim Canadian citizenship simply by writing to the Minister saying they want to be considered Canadians.

Until July 7, 1967, naturalized Canadian citizens, with a few exceptions including spouses and children of native Canadians, forfeited citizenship if they remained abroad for ten consecutive years. But today, naturalized Canadians do not forfeit citizenship because of absence from Canada; they may stay abroad indefinitely.

CHAPTER THIRTEEN

The Three-Stage Citizenship Process

THE APPLICATION

To apply for Canadian citizenship you must be at least 18 years of age and a resident of Canada for three of the four years immediately prior to the application. At least two of the three years of residence must be as a permanent resident. However, half of the time you may have spent in Canada as a visitor, student or even as an illegal immigrant may be counted towards the third year. The three-year residence requirement applies only to the application — those considering citizenship may book the appointment six months before they have the required three-year residence.

Applicants for citizenship must pass national security clearance and have at least a basic knowledge of either

English or French. They must also demonstrate that they have made an effort to learn about Canada and Canadian customs and the responsibilities of a Canadian citizen. A citizenship judge may waive this requirement in the case of elderly persons or others for whom such exemption may be deemed justified.

Citizenship will not be granted to anyone considered a security risk; under a deportation order; on probation or parole; who is an inmate of a prison; or has been convicted of an indictable offence within the three years immediately prior to the application, and anytime after the application and prior to the citizenship ceremony. Time spent in prison, on probation, or on parole is not considered part of the three-year residence requirement.

Those applying for citizenship must present the following documents at the appropriate court of Canadian citizenship (See Appendix 4 for a list of provincial offices):

• A birth certificate or other satisfactory evidence of the date and place of birth. (A passport is acceptable.) At least two additional pieces of identification and satisfactory evidence of permanent resident status are also required.
• Two photographs — black and white or colour — taken within the last year, showing a full front view of head and shoulders without head covering (unless required by religion.) Pictures must be 35 mm x 43 mm (1.4 in. x 1.7 in.) with a 10 mm (0.4 in.) strip at the bottom for your signature. The strip must be signed at the time of handing in the application.

- As well, payment of the application fee must be made at this time. (See Table 10 for a list of citizenship fees.)

THE INTERVIEW

A few weeks before you attend the citizenship ceremony you'll be interviewed by a citizenship judge. This is a brief, private talk, usually lasting no longer than ten minutes. The judge will ask you a few questions about Canada's political system, history and geography and some of the responsibilities of Canadian citizenship. Such questions are based on facts about Canada provided to applicants at the time of the application. The purpose of the interview is simply to determine whether or not you have made an effort to learn about your adopted country.

Table 10
CITIZENSHIP FEES

Category	Cost
Application for citizenship:	
Minors	$35
Adults (18 and over)	$65
Application for proof of citizenship:	
Minors	$15
Adults (18 and over)	$40
(Fees in effect at the time of going to press.)	

Reprinted by permission of Multiculturalism and Citizenship Canada.

THE COURT CEREMONY

Several weeks after the interview, you will be asked to attend the citizenship ceremony. At the ceremony you will take the Oath of Citizenship and receive a citizenship certificate, a wallet-size plastic card. As a souvenir of the occasion, you will also be presented with a larger-size, commemorative paper document, but only the plastic certificate is a legal document.

At the citizenship ceremony you may either "affirm" or "swear" the following Oath of Citizenship:

> *I swear/affirm that I will be faithful and bear true allegiance to Her Majesty Queen Elizabeth the Second, Queen of Canada, Her heirs and Successors, according to law and that I will faithfully observe the laws of Canada and fulfil my duties as a Canadian citizen.*

> *Je jure/déclare solennellement que je serai fidèle et que je porterai sincère allégeance à Sa Majesté la Reine Elizabeth Deux, Reine du Canada, à ses héritiers et à ses successeurs en conformité de la loi et que j'observerai fidèlement les lois du Canada et remplirai mes devoirs de citoyen canadien.*

Before the ceremony is over, you will be asked to sign a copy of the Oath of Citizenship. The ceremony ends with the singing of Canada's national anthem.

Every Canadian may obtain a plastic wallet-size certificate proving he or she is a citizen of Canada. It may be used when applying for a Canadian passport, and for travel to the United States and to some parts of the Caribbean, although a passport is necessary when travelling to most countries. Because there is always the risk of misplacing a passport, a citizenship certificate is very helpful. It can be used to apply for a new passport at a Canadian consulate overseas or to get you back to Canada without the use of a passport.

CHAPTER FOURTEEN

The Nation of Canada

CONFEDERATION TO THE PRESENT DAY

On July 1, 1867, the day of Confederation, the British North America Act (BNA) became law, uniting Canada's first four provinces — Nova Scotia, New Brunswick, Quebec and Ontario — and confirming the parliamentary system as Canada's form of government.

These four provinces merged as one nation primarily to improve their economic and defence position, and to protect their traditions and values from the influence of the United States.

The province of British Columbia joined Confederation in 1871, and Prince Edward Island joined two years later. The Prairie provinces (Manitoba in 1870, Saskatchewan and Alberta in 1905), the Yukon and the

Northwest Territories established provincial boundaries from land acquired by Canada soon after Confederation. Newfoundland became part of Canada much later, in 1949.

In 1867, the British North America Act gave the Canadian government jurisdiction over naturalization and aliens. Naturalization was essentially the process through which foreigners could acquire the rights and privileges bestowed on all British subjects. There was no mention of jurisdiction over citizenship, because only a totally sovereign state could grant the title of citizen to a foreign national residing within its territory. In 1931, the Statute of Westminster recognized Canada's sovereignty, paving the way for the creation of Canada's first Citizenship Act.

Until Canada's first Citizenship Act became law on January 1, 1947, there was no such thing as a citizen of Canada. Thus it wasn't until 80 years after Confederation that the people of Canada could call themselves Canadian citizens! For nationality purposes, Canadian-born and naturalized Canadians were all legally defined as British subjects, both in Canada and abroad.

Indeed, the concept of being British subjects was so cherished that it was retained for 30 years after Canada established its citizenship law. Until a new Citizenship Act took effect February 15, 1977, Canadians were still identified in law and on their passports by the words, "A Canadian citizen is a British subject."

The yearning for a Canadian identity was, perhaps, first sparked shortly after World War I. The war years (1914–18) kindled in Canadians a sense of unity and pride in their country and its achievements. Canada's stunning victory at Vimy Ridge in 1917 is often linked to the country's coming of age in the international arena. In the battle for Vimy Ridge Canadians suffered 10,602 casualties, including 3,598 deaths, but nonetheless, Canadian soldiers succeeded in wrestling Vimy Ridge from the Germans — a feat that British and French troops in two years had failed to accomplish. Canada's role in World War II (1939–45) cemented this desire for a Canadian identity.

It was crucial to establish Canadian citizenship — whether by birth or by choice — in order to guarantee equal status for all Canadians. For Canada is a land of immigrants with a history often carved by foreign affairs. Wars, revolutions, religious persecution, economic upheavals and ethnic strife have brought immigrants of many nationalities and races to Canada's shores.

A large number of Americans, including many of non-British origin, flocked to Canada during the American Revolution when the colonies rebelled against their British masters in 1776. Bestowed with generous land grants, these early American refugees, designated United Empire Loyalists, helped expand Canada's agricultural industry.

Other pre-Confederation immigrants came from Scotland after the Highland clearances, and from Ireland, after the devastating potato famine.

After 1867, as Canada expanded westward, immigrants by the tens of thousands came from the Ukraine, Poland, Germany and other parts of Europe, attracted to the Prairies by the promise of farmland and prosperity.

Others came from Japan and the Indian sub-continent. Large numbers of Chinese immigrants came to Canada, recruited for work gangs to clear the land and lay the tracks that would unite Canada by rail in 1885.

Canada's multicultural identity was actually forged centuries ago. The French began settling in Canada in the early 1600s. By the middle of the 1800s, New France covered much of North America. In 1763, in a Paris treaty in which France ceded most of its North American empire to Britain at the end of the Seven Years' War, the British promised to respect French cultural, religious and language rights in Canada. Unknowingly, that promise heralded the nurturing of a distinct Canadian identity molded by linguistic and cultural diversity.

Since the end of World War II, about six million immigrants have come to Canada. With each new wave of immigrants Canada's makeup changes. Indeed, from the days of the pioneers, the Canadian identity has been made up of many cultural backgrounds — albeit within a French and English framework. Equally a vibrant part of this country's history are Canada's aboriginal peoples, whose communities and cultures trace their roots back thousands of years.

Canadians of diverse ethnic backgrounds and racial origins are all part of the multicultural umbrella now defined in law, and enshrined in the Constitution Act of 1982 as part of the Charter of Rights and Freedoms.

FACTS ABOUT CANADA

The following list of facts provides a good introduction to the history, culture, geography and political system of Canada:

- The Royal Canadian Mounted Police were originally called the Northwest Mounted Police, founded in 1873.

- The St. Lawrence Seaway, an inland navigation system of rivers, canals and lakes, extends 3,769 kilometres (2,343 miles). It is the longest waterway of its kind in the world.

- The Mackenzie–Peace River, beginning in Alberta and flowing through the Northwest Territories to the Beaufort Sea, is 4,241 kilometres (2,635 miles) long.

- The Trans–Canada Highway, stretching for 7,821 kilometres (4,860 miles) is the world's longest roadway.

- The snowmobile, basketball, Standard Time, the telephone and the electron microscope are all Canadian inventions.

- Canada's name is derived from the Huron–Iroquois word *Kanata* meaning "village." Legend has it that Jacques Cartier appropriated the word in 1515 when aboriginal people used it to describe the site that was to become Quebec City.

- There are 53 aboriginal languages in Canada.

- Four provinces have names derived from aboriginal languages: Ontario (Iroquois, *knanadario*) meaning "beautiful waters"; Quebec (Algonquin, *kebek*) meaning "narrow passage"; Manitoba (Cree, *manito-wapow*) meaning "strait of the Great Spirit"; and Saskatchewan (Cree, *Ksiiskatchewan Sipi*) meaning "swift flowing river."

- There are six time zones spanning Canada from the Atlantic to the Pacific coast.

- The first Canadian postage stamp was the three-penny beaver stamp designed by Sir Sandford Fleming. It was issued on April 25, 1851. Fleming, Canada's foremost railway surveyor and nineteenth-century construction engineer, successfully proposed in Washington the adoption of Standard Time in 1884.

- Most of Canada's legal system is based on British Common Law. Quebec's legal system is derived from the old French civil law and the subsequent Napoleonic code adopted in France.

- Canada is both a democracy and a constitutional monarchy.

- The head of state is the Queen of Canada, who is also Queen of Britain, Australia and New Zealand and a host of other countries. Although every act of government in Canada is instituted in the name of the Queen, laws are drafted by Canadians.

- No elected person in Canada above the rank of mayor has a definite term of office. Members of Parliament or of a provincial legislature may be removed from office in a short time if the government is defeated in the House of Commons or a provincial legislature on a motion of censure or a non-confidence vote.

- Every province has its own legislative assembly that is similar to the House of Commons.

- Municipal governments are set up by the provinces. They are responsible for a wide range of local services including water supply, sewage and garbage disposal, roads, street lighting, building codes, libraries, parks and playgrounds. There are about 5,000 municipal governments in Canada.

- The Canadian Charter of Rights and Freedoms guarantees that all Canadian citizens have:
  — The right to vote in federal and provincial elections.
  — The right to be a candidate in federal and provincial elections.
  — The right to enter, remain or leave Canada.
  — The right to work and reside in any province.
  — The right to an English or French language education.

(For more facts about Canada see Table 11 and Appendices 5 and 6.)

Table 11
FACTS ABOUT CANADA

Area
Land: 9,167,165 sq.km.
Fresh Water: 755,165 sq.km.
Total: (land and lakes) 9,922,330 sq.km.
Population: 27.5 million
Capital: Ottawa.

Province	Population	Capital City
Newfoundland	575,000	St. John's
Prince Edward Island	130,000	Charlottetown
Nova Scotia	900,000	Halifax
New Brunswick	725,000	Fredericton
Quebec	7,000,000	Quebec City
Ontario	10,100,000	Toronto
Manitoba	1,100,000	Winnipeg
Saskatchewan	950,000	Regina
Alberta	2,600,000	Edmonton
British Columbia	3,500,000	Victoria
Yukon Territory	28,000	Whitehorse
Northwest Territories	58,000	Yellowknife

Reprinted by permission of Multiculturalism and Citizenship Canada.

CANADA'S FLAG

For more than 300 years, the people of Canada have used the maple leaf as a symbol for the country. The maple leaf was used in the design of coins, stamps, banners and shields, but was not adopted as part of Canada's national flag until 98 years after Confederation.

Indeed, it was under the British Union Jack — declared Canada's official flag in 1911 — that Canadians fought overseas in World War I. In 1924, the Red Ensign was adopted to identify Canada at home and abroad.

However, after red and white were proclaimed Canada's official colours in 1921, some politicians began calling for a Canadian flag. The controversial debate dragged on for more than 40 years, intensifying with the imminent approach of Canada's centennial year in 1967. By 1964, a special all-party parliamentary committee was assigned the task of selecting a design from more than 2,000 suggested by Canadians from coast to coast.

The winning design was a single red maple leaf on a white background framed by two red borders. It was based on a design submitted by George Stanley, a Calgary-born historian, educator and soldier. Stanley served as lieutenant-governor of New Brunswick from 1982 to 1987 and, in the early 1960s, was Dean of Arts at Kingston's Royal Military Institute.

When the Canadian flag was first introduced, there was widespread criticism and charges that it was an insult to Canada's British heritage. However, in Quebec, where the Red Ensign had been viewed as a symbol of British domination, the Maple Leaf flag was warmly embraced by the majority of people as a symbol of Canada. The Canadian flag was officially raised for the first time on February 15, 1965.

CANADA'S ANTHEM: O CANADA

O Canada! Our home and native land!
True patriot love in all thy sons command.
With glowing hearts we see thee rise,
The True North strong and free!
From far and wide, O Canada,
We stand on guard for thee.
God keep our land glorious and free!
O Canada, we stand on guard for thee.
O Canada, we stand on guard for thee.

O Canada! Terre de nos aïeux,
Ton front est ceint de fleurons glorieux!
Car ton bras sait porter l'épée,
Il sait porter la croix!
Ton histoire est une épopée
Des plus brillants exploits.
Et ta valeur, de foi trempée,
Protégera nos foyers et nos droits,
Protégera nos foyers et nos droits.

Sir Adolphe-Basile Routhier wrote the original "O Canada" lyrics in French and Calixa Lavallée wrote the music. It was first sung in public at a banquet in Quebec City in 1880.

Many English versions have appeared over the years. The version on which the official English lyrics are based was written in 1908 by Mr. Justice Robert Stanley Weir. The official English version includes changes recommended in 1968 by a Special Joint Committee of the Senate and House of Commons. The French lyrics have remained the same.

PART THREE

Questions and Answers

Questions and
Answers

As a reporter for *The Toronto Star*, specializing in minority issues and immigration matters, I became increasingly aware of the confusion immigrants often experienced in dealing with government agencies and complex immigration and citizenship laws.

I began writing a weekly column in 1982 dealing specifically with topics of particular interest to immigrants trying to make their way through bureaucratic red tape and the maze of government services and regulations.

Indeed, citizenship laws can be very confusing, and those considering Canadian citizenship are advised to first discuss their plans with their respective consulates. Older Canadians born abroad are often shocked to discover they must apply for immigrant visas to spend their retirement years in their country of birth.

The following collection of questions and answers is based on the tens of thousands of letters I have received over the years, dealing with sponsorships, immigrant visas, government pensions, the citizenship process and laws of other countries that may continue to apply to Canadian residents born abroad.

Q: We emigrated from Turkey several years ago and we're all Canadian citizens now. Our 18-year-old son wants to go home for a holiday. Is there any risk involved?

A: He should cancel that trip to Turkey. Your son is a dual citizen and eligible for military conscription in Turkey. Canadian-born children of Turkish parents are exempt from military duty, but those born in Turkey remain eligible for the armed forces should they set foot in Turkey again. There is a provision that allows Turkish nationals to reduce the length of military service by paying a fee. However, a minimum two-month stint in the armed forces is still mandatory. Turkish nationals in Canada on student visas or for temporary employment may postpone their military service by applying to the Turkish embassy in Ottawa. Write to: Embassy of Turkey, Citizens' Affairs, 197 Wurtemburg Street, Ottawa, Ontario, Canada K1N 8L9.

Q: My mother is Italian-born. My father is French. I was born in Canada. Do I have a claim to Italian citizenship?

A: Previously, only fathers could pass on Italian citizenship. But the law was changed and citizenship may also be claimed when only the mother is Italian. The change in the law was made retroactive to 1948.

Q: My brother is a U.S. citizen and a pensioner. His American wife is not of pension age yet. What must he do so they may live in Canada?

A: If they're Americans, period, they must apply for an immigrant visa like everyone else. You can't sponsor them. If your brother is a Canadian who embraced American citizenship after February 14, 1977, he has retained Canadian citizenship; he is a dual citizen. He may return to Canada at will and he may sponsor his wife for permanent resident status. If he became a U.S. citizen prior to February 15, 1977, he lost his Canadian citizenship under the old law. Effective on that date, citizenship is no longer forfeited by taking the citizenship of another country. But the change in the law recognizing dual and multiple citizenship was not made retroactive. Thus, he is deemed a foreigner, for immigration purposes. The federal government, however, recognizes such ties with Canada, and visa officers are directed to "consider sympathetically" applications for visas from former Canadian citizens.

Q: I am an American citizen and a permanent resident in Canada. As a taxpayer, do I have a vote in Canadian elections? Will I get the old-age pension at age 65? As a U.S. citizen, will I be entitled to bring to Canada, duty-free, some furniture my relatives in the U.S. wish to give to me?

A: You don't have a vote when not a Canadian citizen, but you will collect the Old Age Security Pension. Canadian residence takes precedence over citizenship. You have no special claim to duty-free goods from the U.S.

However, in the case of an inheritance, furniture, paintings and other articles may be brought to Canada duty-free. Alert Canada Customs.

Q: I was born in Toronto in 1915 and I've never lived outside Canada. In 1937, I married a U.S. citizen. Some years ago I applied for a Canadian passport, but to my horror I was told I was not a Canadian. To add insult to injury, I discovered that my neighbour, born in Britain, has been given a Canadian passport, although she insists she's never applied for Canadian citizenship. She says it was bestowed on her because she had married a Canadian soldier during the war. Can you please tell me how this can be so?
A: Yes. It's true. You're not a Canadian. But you may regain Canadian citizenship by simply informing the Citizenship Court office that you want to be considered a Canadian.

Here's the reason for the confusion. Prior to January 1, 1947, when Canada's first Citizenship Act became law, Canadian citizens as such, did not exist. They were British subjects for nationality purposes. At the time, Canadian women who married non-British subjects automatically forfeited their British subject status. Thus, when you married an American, you ceased to be a British subject.

On January 1, 1947, Canada's first Citizenship Act automatically bestowed Canadian citizenship on all British subjects who had been in Canada five years or longer, and on foreign women married to Canadians who had become Canadian residents prior to

January 1, 1947. Thus, because you had lost British subject status, you didn't qualify for automatic Canadian citizenship. Your neighbor, married to a Canadian and living in Canada prior to January 1, 1947, automatically gained Canadian citizenship on that date.

Q: I was born in England in 1921, moved to Australia in 1937, and later became an Australian citizen. Later still, I returned to Britain. After the war I came to Canada and became a citizen in 1957. I have a son in Australia and wondered whether I would have any problem joining him in Queensland. Am I entitled to an Australian passport? If I returned to Australia for good, would I forfeit Canadian citizenship? Can I live in Britain if I choose to do so someday?
A: You lost Australian citizenship when you took Canadian citizenship, but, you remained a British citizen. You may return to Britain anytime. If you wish to live in Australia, you may have your son sponsor you. You would remain a Canadian regardless of how long you remained abroad, or whether you regained Australian citizenship someday. Before February 15, 1977, Canadian citizenship was lost in taking the citizenship of another country, but not any more. And for some time, those who remained abroad ten consecutive years or more automatically forfeited Canadian citizenship. That law was repealed in 1967.

Q: If my application for permanent residence is accepted for processing from within Canada, how long will it take to obtain permanent resident status?

A: You should obtain permanent resident status in about 18 to 24 months.

Q: When can I work?
A: You may obtain a work permit when the application has been approved in principle, usually in about four months after the application is filed. However, until you have passed your medical examination you will not be permitted to work in a job where public health is a concern, including restaurants, fast-food outlets and cafeterias.

Q: When can I attend school?
A: You may attend school once "approval in principle" is granted.

Q: Do I need permission to remain in Canada while I am waiting for permanent resident status?
A: Your visitor status must be kept up to date. To let it expire means you are in Canada illegally. Hence, more problems with Immigration, and a greater delay in gaining permanent resident status. To stay in legal status you must apply in writing to an immigration centre. You must pay the required fee. However, after that, no more fees will be demanded for such extensions during the processing period.

Q: Will I have to attend an interview by Immigration?
A: In most cases, no. However, there may be reason to require an interview to further investigate your case. Thus, the more thorough and complete the information

provided in the application, the less likely you'd be called in for an interview and further investigation.

Q: I was born in Jamaica. In 1957, at the age of 10, I moved to England and lived there until 1975, when I came to Canada. I am now a Canadian citizen. My daughter, however, was born and lives in Britain and would like me to join her there. Is it true that I can't return to England, because after Jamaica gained independence I became a Jamaican citizen, and therefore have no claim to British citizenship?
A: Jamaica gained independence from Britain on August 6, 1962. Your British citizenship depends on just *when* in 1957 you moved to England. If you lived in Britain a full five years prior to Jamaican independence you may have a claim to British citizenship, and you should ask the nationality division of the British High Commission in Ottawa to determine your status. Their phone number is: (613) 237-1303.

Q: Apparently, the Italian government has made some changes in the law concerning citizenship and the military draft. How does this affect me? I was born in Toronto of Italian citizen parents. I believe I have dual citizenship.
A: Until recently, the military draft in Italy applied to all males aged 18 to 26. For those who left Italy after age 17, military obligations remained until age 28. Now, the military draft applies to all those aged 18 to 26, both Italian immigrants and dual citizens. Because you were

born in Canada of Italian parents you are a dual citizen and eligible for the draft if you establish residence in Italy. However, if you have good reason to remain in Italy for an extended period — including university studies — you may be granted a certificate of exemption from military service. If you are going on a short holiday, you are advised to apply for clearance by Italian consulate officials. It removes the risk of a hassle with *carabinieri* who may mistake you for a draft dodger.

Q: I have two grandsons in India aged two and one. My son has a drug problem and can't look after them properly. My wife and I are Canadian citizens. Can we adopt them and sponsor them to come to Canada? We could really help them this way.

A: Unless the circumstances are unusual, child welfare authorities in Canada will not approve an adoption in Canada when at least one parent is still alive. Hence, you may have a better chance of adopting your grandchildren through the courts in India. You don't say whether the children's mother is still alive, or whether she has left the family. If she's alive, the children should be with their mother. You can help your grandchildren by financially supporting your daughter-in-law, so that she may properly provide for the children when your son can't or won't.

Q: I was born in Germany, my husband in Iran. He is now a Canadian citizen but I've remained a German national. My question concerns our eight-year-old son, who was born in Germany. For business reasons we may be returning indefinitely to

Germany. I want my son to have Canadian citizenship so that he'll always have the right to return to Canada. But in doing so, would he lose his German citizenship?

A: You son may become a dual citizen only if you apply for Canadian citizenship and include him in the application. But then, you would lose your citizenship of Germany. German nationals who take the citizenship of another country automatically lose their German citizenship. But this does not apply to minors who gain a foreign citizenship because of the actions of their parents. Minors can lose their German citizenship only if their parents take the unusual step of asking the courts in Germany to withdraw it.

Some parents do this to spare their children from military obligations, should they take up permanent residence in Germany or any member country of the European Economic Community. Canadians who also have German citizenship are exempted from German military obligations and may take holidays to Germany but fear being drafted. By the way, your son is German only because you are. Unlike Canadian citizenship law, one's birth on German soil doesn't bestow German nationality. Indeed, until January 1, 1975, German citizenship could only be acquired through one's German father. But now, German nationality is acquired when either parent is a German citizen.

Q: If a person has a "certificate of entitlement" to live in Britain, does this mean he or she is a British citizen? Does this effectively make the person's passport a dual passport? Would my parents be able

to revalidate their British citizenship by obtaining a "right of abode" certificate? Their passports, in which I was included as "offspring born in Canada," have long since expired. Is clearance by British authorities in Canada required before I can move to Britain for a few years?

A: None of you needs permission to live in Britain; you're all British citizens. British citizenship isn't lost when you become a Canadian citizen. Hence, your parents remain British. They're dual citizens. And you're considered a British citizen because you are the offspring of British-born parents. You may all hold both Canadian and British passports.

A "certificate of entitlement" is required for those born of a British-born mother prior to January 1, 1983, and who were either over 18 when the law was changed, bestowing citizenship through either parent, or if they otherwise failed to apply for British citizenship before they became 18.

A "clearance" certificate is available for those without a claim to British citizenship but with close links to Britain, such as those who have at least one British-born grandparent. The clearance permit allows such persons to live and work in Britain for a renewable four-year period.

Q: I have a fiancée in the Philippines. We want to get married over there so that all her relatives may attend the wedding festivities. What must I do to make sure that after the honeymoon we can fly to Canada together as husband and wife?

A: Apply as soon as possible to sponsor your intended bride. It's a good idea to discuss your wedding plans with immigration officials. For those who do not require visitor visas to come to Canada, it's not such a problem because visitors may be sponsored from within Canada. An intended bride could decide to get married once in Canada, and then she would be able to stay here, but Filipinos must obtain visas to travel to Canada. If the visa office is aware she intends to get married and stay in Canada, chances are they won't give her a visitor visa. They'd want her to be processed through normal channels in the Philippines.

Q: I am a refugee claimant married to a Canadian citizen. I am to be processed for permanent resident status on humanitarian and compassionate grounds. My problem is that two years ago I got drunk and walked out of a store without paying for some things. I was convicted of theft but didn't receive a jail sentence. Will this affect my sponsorship?
A: You didn't get a jail term so this suggests that it was a minor theft, and was processed by the court as a summary rather than indictible offence. In Canada such a crime may be processed either way at the discretion of the prosecution. A summary conviction will not affect your application for permanent residence.

However, if the conviction had been by a court ouside Canada, it would be considered an indictible offence regardless of how it was processed by the court of the other country. In such a case, you wouldn't be eligible for sponsorship until at least five years had passed since the conviction, or until the sentence had ended. And then you'd have to produce character references vouching for your rehabilitation.

Q: My mother came to Canada in 1952 from the Republic of Ireland and has lived in this country ever since. She's now about to start collecting the Canadian old-age pension, but was wondering whether she may also be entitled to a pension from Ireland?

A: Irish pensions are adjusted according to residence, employment and pension contributions. Each case is considered on its own merits. The good news is that if your mother fails to meet the normal requirements for the Irish pension, she may qualify for benefits nonetheless, under an agreement on pensions between Canada and the Emerald Isle, which allows the combination of residences in both countries to satisfy each country's residence requirement. To apply, write to: Department of Social Welfare, Aras Mhic Dhiarmada, Dublin 1, Republic of Ireland.

Q: My maternal grandparents were both Scottish and my mother was born in Scotland. She married an Englishman and I was born in Canada. My parents were divorced around the time I was born and I don't know my father. Am I eligible for a British passport?

A: Since your father was British-born you are considered a British citizen and therefore are entitled to a British passport. In order to obtain one you'll have to produce your father's birth certificate, your parents' marriage certificate and your birth certificate (all in long form). To obtain your father's birth certificate, write to : General Register Office, Room 9, Smedley Hydro, Trafalgar Road, Southport, Merseyside, PR8 2HH,

England. Give your father's full name, place and date of birth, and if possible, full name of his parents and his mother's maiden name.

Q: I was born in Canada of Dutch immigrants who never became Canadian citizens. In 1963, when I was six months old we moved to the United States. In 1969, my parents applied for American citizenship and I became a U.S. citizen. I'd like to move back to Canada. Am I a dual citizen?
A: Yes. But only because your father was not a Canadian. Under Canadian law in effect at the time (revoked in 1977), you would have forfeited Canadian citizenship if your father had "ceased to be a Canadian" by embracing the citizenship of another country. However, your father couldn't have ceased to be a Canadian as he never was one. Therefore, you never lost Canadian citizenship.

Q: My husband and I will be going to Australia for a couple of years. We may remain there. Will our children born there be dual citizens? How soon would we qualify for Australian citizenship?
A: Effective August 20, 1986, Australian citizenship is acquired at birth only if at least one parent is a citizen of Australia or is a permanent resident. Thus, whether your children would be dual citizens depends on your status in Australia at the time of their birth. Immigrants may apply for Australian citizenship after two years as permanent residents.

Q: My wife and I are Canadian citizens and live in Toronto. Since I have no son, I am longing to

adopt one of my sister's sons. He is 19 and living in China. I can well afford to support him. What must I do to bring him to Canada?

A: Forget it. Only children adopted before age 13 may be sponsored. The age cut-off was introduced several years ago, because Canadian residents were exploiting the adoption process by bringing to Canada relatives who otherwise didn't qualify to immigrate.

Q: What must I do to legally change my name? I plan to go away this summer and I want to obtain a new passport under a new surname. Do I need a lawyer? Is it expensive? How long will it take?

A: You don't need a lawyer. A change of name is an administrative process, costing $137. Normally it takes 10 months to obtain a name change, but, for good reason, it may be processed much more quickly. To apply, or obtain more information write to: Registrar General Branch, P.O. Box 4600, 189 Red River Road, Thunder Bay, Ontario P7B 6L8. In Metro Toronto, applications may be made in person at 950 Bay Street (second floor).

Q: I was born in Britain. My husband and son were born in Canada. Our son is 17 and may claim British citizenship provided he does so before he is 18. If he becomes a dual citizen, is there a risk of his being drafted in the British army should he visit England when he is of military age?

A: There is no military draft in Britain. The National Service was discontinued shortly after the end of the Korean War.

Q: I am a 53-year-old woman who has lived in Canada for 20 years. I am a Canadian citizen. I have no relatives in this country but my brother has an illegitimate daughter who would like to join me. May I sponsor her?

A: Those who have no family here may sponsor one close relative regardless of age, provided they have no other sponsorable family member. It makes no difference that your brother's daughter is illegitimate. But if you have a spouse, child or parent in your country of birth, you can't sponsor your brother's daughter.

Q: I am an immigrant from an Arab country. I would like to return but my wife refuses to go. She doesn't have a job, money or family here. If I go, doesn't she have to come with me?

A: No, she doesn't. You can't force your wife to leave Canada. If you leave her penniless, she'll be given welfare assistance.

Q: I was born in Canada in 1961. At the time of my birth my parents were Austrian citizens. Am I entitled to dual citizenship? Would I be able to work in Austria? My mother contributed to the pension plan in Austria from 1949 to 1958. Would she be entitled to a partial pension from Austria?

A: You have a claim to Austrian citizenship. Thus, you may live and work in Austria provided you go there with an Austrian passport. Until August 31, 1983, Austrian citizenship could be acquired only when the father was Austrian. Now citizenship is automatically bestowed on children who have either an Austrian mother or father. In addition, those born of a foreign father and an Austrian mother and were under 19 years of age on September 1, 1983, have a claim to Austrian citizenship.

Normally, applicants for the Austrian pension must have contributed to the pension plan in Austria for 15 years to collect benefits when living in Canada. However, your mother may qualify for an Austrian pension under the Canada–Austria agreement on pensions, which allows for the combination of residences in both countries to satisfy basic pension eligibility conditions of both Canada and Austria. More details may be obtained through any Income Security Programs office or Canadian consulate.

Q: A friend in my country of birth is thinking of retiring to Canada. He is a wealthy businessman from an Islamic country who would probably qualify as an investor. My friend, a Muslim, has two wives and several children from each of his wives. Would both wives and all the children be allowed to come to Canada with him?

A: He may bring to Canada all of his unmarried children under 19 — and older if still totally dependent on him. But only his first wife may be considered his spouse. In Canada's eyes she's his only legal wife. However, his second wife may, at Immigration's discretion be allowed to come to Canada on humanitarian and compassionate grounds.

Q: I have a son back home. I send money, clothing and other gifts to him, but I don't support his mother. We're not married and she has her own

source of income. Can I claim my child as a deduction for income tax purposes?
A: Yes, you can, but only if the child is wholly dependent on you. Christmas presents and other occasional gifts to the child won't entitle you to a tax deduction.

Q: My daughter was born just outside Seoul, South Korea, to an American soldier. She needs a birth certificate for U.S. citizenship purposes. Where can she apply for one in Korea?
A: Although born in Korea, your daughter is not a Korean national because her father was a foreigner. In Korea only births of nationals are registered. Your daughter was probably registered by her soldier father as an American born abroad. To obtain a birth certificate she should write to: Correspondents' Branch, Passport Services, Department of State, Washington, D.C., 20524 U.S.A. Include as much pertinent information as possible related to her father's posting in Korea, and specify when and where she was born. There's a U.S. $4 fee.

Q: I was born in Canada. So was my mother. But my mother's father was born in Dublin. I'd like to visit Ireland and perhaps work there for some time. What visa do I need and how do I apply?
A: The Irish Nationality and Citizenship Act grants citizenship to those born outside Ireland who have at least one Irish-born grandparent. Thus, you have a claim to Irish citizenship and you may live and work there. To obtain the necessary forms to apply for Irish citizenship write to: Embassy of Ireland, 170 Metcalfe Street, Ottawa, Canada K2P 1P3.

Q: My son, a professional engineer, has been working outside Canada for the last 11 years. He has lived in Algeria, Saudi Arabia, Libya and now Egypt. He wants to come back to Canada with his family, but Canadian authorities in Cairo are giving him a hard time. In 1988, my son married a Filipino, a mother of four children aged 11 to 16. They were married in New York because the Canadian visa office in Egypt wouldn't let his intended wife travel to Canada for the wedding. For more than a year he's been trying to obtain the necessary visas for his family to come to Canada, but he's been told his family cannot be considered genuine immigrants to Canada. Is it significant that his wife is a Roman Catholic and her divorce was obtained in Guam? If the marriage in New York is legal, why are Canadian authorities also questioning his marital status? It seems Canadian law recognizes common-law relationships, but not marriages that take place in New York. Please clarify.

A: Your son probably wanted his family to accompany him to Canada as visitors, so that he could seek to sponsor them from within Canada on compassionate grounds, rather than returning to Canada alone to sponsor them — a process that could take as long as two years. The visa office likely told him his family couldn't be considered genuine visitors since they had no intention of returning to Egypt; they expect his family to go through normal channels in Cairo. There may have been other problems as well. The marriage, albeit legal in New York, may not be acceptable to Canadian

Immigration. Immigration and family law can be quite confusing. For example, Ontario law recognizes common-law relationships, but federal immigration law does not. A "quickie" divorce in Guam would not be recognized by Immigration unless your daughter-in-law was a resident in the jurisdiction of the Guam court when the divorce decree was issued.

Indeed, she may have to ask the courts in the Philippines to annul her marriage, before Canada will recognize her as your son's wife. Until a few years ago, divorce was impossible in the Philippines, but that's changed now. A new family law, effective August 4, 1988, permits the voiding of a marriage on the grounds of "psychological incapacity to comply with the essential marital obligations," even when such a problem may not be identified until much later in married life.

Q: My wife and I would like to travel to Lebanon on Canadian passports. I was born in Lebanon but now I am a Canadian citizen. My wife, however, is American. Does she forfeit her U.S. citizenship when she takes Canadian citizenship and applies for a Canadian passport?

A: No. Not any more. Previously, those who took the citizenship of another country had to satisfy the U.S. government that there was never the intent to renounce U.S. citizenship. Now it's the other way around. Such persons are automatically deemed to have remained U.S. citizens — unless they formally renounce American citizenship in front of a U.S. consular officer, or their conduct strongly suggests a wish to relinquish American citizenship. The change of policy is based on the premise that U.S. citizens intend to retain their citizenship even "when they obtain naturalization in a foreign state, subscribe to routine declarations of allegiance to a foreign state, or accept non- policy level employment with a foreign government."

Those who lost their U.S. citizenship under the previous law may now regain it and become dual citizens. To have their cases reconsidered, they should apply to a U.S. consulate, or write directly to: Director, Office of Citizens Consular Services, Room 4811 NS, Department of State, Washington, D.C. 20520.

Q: I am a Canadian citizen who was born in the United Kingdom. I understand I may hold passports to both countries. Is there any legal ramification when travelling with two passports? Do I need a citizenship card to apply for a Canadian passport or can I just send the large paper certificate I was given when I became a citizen? Is the paper certificate still valid or must it be the wallet-size plastic kind?

A: You may legally hold both UK and Canadian passports. Prior to February 15, 1977, new citizens were presented with paper certificates. Plastic wallet-size cards were available on request. Since February 15, 1977, only plastic certificates have been given out; citizens still receive a commemorative paper document, but this is not a legal certificate, only a souvenir. Thus, if you gained Canadian citizenship prior to February 15, 1977, you hold a legal paper document that's still valid for passport purposes. Otherwise, you must produce a plastic certificate to obtain a Canadian passport.

Q: I am a dual citizen, German and Canadian, of military age in Germany. Is there any risk of being drafted if I go to Germany for a holiday?

A: No. German nationals living outside Germany are exempt from military obligations in that country.

Q: I was born in Germany of German parents and immigrated to Great Britain in 1938. In 1948 I became a naturalized British citizen. Nine years later I immigrated to Canada and became a Canadian citizen. My wife is Canadian-born. What citizenships do I hold? Is our son, who was born in 1958, entitled to a British passport?

A: You have Canadian and British citizenships, but not German. That was lost when you became a British citizen. Your son has no claim to British citizenship because you are not British-born.

Conclusion

I hope this book has helped you to better understand some of the more confusing laws, regulations and policies affecting immigration and citizenship in Canada. I have tried to cut through the legalese of both immigration and citizenship, and to eliminate the red tape that you may encounter in dealing with an impersonal government bureaucracy.

This book includes the most recent amendments to the 1976 Immigration Act, amendments which became effective January 31, 1993. The new bill sparked a lot of controversy and became law only after the federal government considered presentations and briefs from a large number of individuals and from groups representing millions of Canadians.

The most controversial aspects of the new immigration law include the fingerprinting and photographing of refugee claimants; denying access to refugee

claimants coming to Canada from so-called safe countries; and requiring some immigrants to live in specific
parts of Canada for a while. There was also much
debate over inadmissibility provisions, later amended,
which would have denied entry to Canada for omis-
sions or acts, which, while considered crimes in
Canada, are not so in the countries where they
occurred; and to people who although they have
belonged, or currently are members of organizations
involved in criminal activities, themselves are not
engaged in criminal activities.

Those in favour of the changes insisted that widespread abuse of the immigration system made them
necessary. However, critics of the bill voiced concern
about the violation of individual rights. In the end,
while the changes were essentially kept, the Immigration Minister did agree to soften parts of the bill.

Of course, Canada's immigration policy puts Canada
and Canadians first by controlling the immigration flow
to meet national and regional population goals and
work force needs, while also safeguarding the health
and security of Canadians. Nonetheless, Canada's immigration and citizenship policies will clearly continue to
offer people from all over the world, regardless of ethnic or racial origin, the opportunity to immigrate here
and become Canadian citizens.

Appendices

Appendix 1
COUNTRIES OF ORIGIN OF THE TOP TEN IMMIGRANT
GROUPS EACH YEAR SINCE 1968

1968

Britain	32,031
U.S.A.	20,846
W. Germany	8,969
France	8,188
Austria	8,059
Portugal	7,768
Greece	7,749
Hong Kong	7,611
Yugoslavia	4,665
Switzerland	3,524
TOP TEN	109,410
ALL SOURCES	184,380

1969

Britain	62,274
U.S.A.	22,893
Hong Kong	7,642
Portugal	7,220
Greece	6,987
W. Germany	5,969
Trinidad & Tobago	5,627
France	5,580
India	5,470
Jamaica	3,903
TOP TEN	133,565
ALL SOURCES	162,997

1970

Britain	26,490
U.S.A.	26,423
Portugal	7,902
Yugoslavia	7,670
Greece	6,324
India	5,649
Hong Kong	4,508
Jamaica	4,418
France	4,402
Trinidad & Tobago	4,289
TOP TEN	98,075
ALL SOURCES	147,589

1971

U.SA.	24,370
Britain	15,451
Portugal	9,157
Italy	5,790
India	5,311
Hong Kong	5,309
Philippines	4,781
Greece	4,769
Trinidad & Tobago	4,149
Jamaica	3,903
TOP TEN	82,990
ALL SOURCES	121,901

1972

Britain	18,197
U.S.A.	15,571
Portugal	8,737
Hong Kong	6,297
India	5,049
Uganda	5,021
Kampuchea	4,593
Greece	4,016
Philippines	3,948
Jamaica	3,092
TOP TEN	74,521
ALL SOURCES	122,006

1973

Britain	26,973
U.S.A.	25,242
Hong Kong	14,662
Portugal	13,483
Jamaica	9,363
India	9,203
Philippines	6,757
Greece	5,833
Italy	5,468
Trinidad & Tobago	5,138
TOP TEN	122,122
ALL SOURCES	184,200

1974

Britain	38,546
U.S.A.	20,541
Portugal	16,333
India	12,868
Hong Kong	12,704
Jamaica	11,286
Philippines	9,564
Greece	5,632
Kampuchea	5,226
Haiti	4,857
TOP TEN	137,557
ALL SOURCES	218,465

1975

Britain	34,978
U.S.A.	20,155
Hong Kong	11,132
India	10,144
Portugal	8,457
Jamaica	8,211
Philippines	7,364
Guyana	4,394
Korea	4,331
Greece	4,062
TOP TEN	113,228
ALL SOURCES	187,881

1976

Britain	21,548
U.S.A.	17,315
Hong Kong	10,725
Jamaica	7,282
India	6,733
Portugal	5,344
Italy	4,530
Guyana	3,430
France	3,281
Philippines	2,939
TOP TEN	83,127
ALL SOURCES	149,429

1977

Britain	17,997
U.S.A.	12,888
Hong Kong	6,371
Jamaica	6,291
Philippines	6,232
India	5,555
Lebanon	3,847
Portugal	3,579
Italy	3,411
France	2,757
TOP TEN	68,928
ALL SOURCES	114,914

1978

Britain	11,801
U.S.A.	9,945
India	5,110
Hong Kong	4,740
Philippines	4,370
Italy	3,976
Jamaica	3,858
Portugal	3,086
Haiti	1,782
France	1,754
TOP TEN	50,422
ALL SOURCES	86,313

1979

Vietnam	19,859
Britain	12,853
U.S.A.	9,617
Hong Kong	5,966
India	4,517
Laos	3,903
Philippines	3,873
Portugal	3,783
Jamaica	3,213
Guyana	2,473
TOP TEN	70,057
ALL SOURCES	112,096

1980

Vietnam	25,541
Britain	18,245
U.S.A.	9,926
India	8,483
Hong Kong	6,309
Laos	6,266
Philippines	6,051
China	4,936
Portugal	4,104
Kampuchea	3,265
TOP TEN	93,126
ALL SOURCES	143,717

1981

Britain	21,110
U.S.A.	10,559
India	8,256
Vietnam	8,251
China	6,550
Hong Kong	6,451
Philippines	5,859
Haiti	3,667
Portugal	3,265
Poland	3,050
TOP TEN	77,018
ALL SOURCES	128,618

1982

Britain	16,431
U.S.A.	9,360
Poland	8,728
India	7,776
Hong Kong	6,542
Vietnam	5,935
Philippines	5,062
W. Germany	4,425
China	3,571
Guyana	3,486
TOP TEN	71,316
ALL SOURCES	121,147

1983

U.S.A.	7,381
India	7,041
Hong Kong	6,711
Vietnam	6,451
Britain	5,737
Philippines	4,454
Haiti	2,827
Guyana	2,605
El Salvador	2,551
W. Germany	2,518
TOP TEN	48,276
ALL SOURCES	89,157

1984

Vietnam	10,950
Hong Kong	7,696
U.S.A.	6,922
India	5,502
Poland	4,499
Philippines	3,748
El Salvador	2,579
Jamaica	2,479
China	2,214
Britain	2,104
TOP TEN	48,693
ALL SOURCES	88,239

1985

Vietnam	10,404
Hong Kong	7,380
U.S.A.	6,669
Britain	4,454
India	4,028
Poland	3,617
Philippines	3,076
Jamaica	2,922
El Salvador	2,881
Guyana	2,301
TOP TEN	47,732
ALL SOURCES	84,302

1986

U.S.A.	7,275
India	6,940
Vietnam	6,622
Hong Kong	5,983
Poland	5,231
Britain	5,088
Jamaica	4,652
Philippines	4,102
Guyana	3,905
El Salvador	3,167
TOP TEN	52,965
ALL SOURCES	99,219

1987

Hong Kong	23,281
India	10,409
Britain	9,231
U.S.A.	9,172
Philippines	8,310
Portugal	6,537
Poland	6,467
Guyana	6,196
Vietnam	3,923
Jamaica	3,669
TOP TEN	87,195
ALL SOURCES	152,098

1988

Hong Kong	23,281
India	10,409
Poland	9,231
Britain	9,172
Philippines	8,310
U.S.A.	6,537
Portugal	6,467
Vietnam	6,196
Jamaica	3,923
Iran	3,669
TOP TEN	87,195
ALL SOURCES	161,829

1989

Hong Kong	19,908
Poland	15,985
Philippines	11,393
Vietnam	9,425
India	8,819
Britain	8,420
Portugal	8,189
U.S.A.	6,881
Lebanon	6,179
China	4,430
TOP TEN	99,629
ALL SOURCES	192,001

1990

Hong Kong	29,261
Poland	16,579
Lebanon	12,462
Philippines	12,042
India	10,624
Vietnam	9,081
Britain	8,217
China	7,989
Portugal	7,917
U.S.A.	6,084
TOP TEN	120,256
ALL SOURCES	214,230

1991

Hong Kong	22,340
Poland	15,731
China	13,915
India	12,848
Philippines	12,335
Lebanon	11,987
Vietnam	8,963
Britain	7,543
El Salvador	6,977
Sri Lanka	6,826
TOP TEN	119,465
ALL SOURCES	230,781

1992*

Hong Kong	31,309
Sri Lanka	9,424
India	9,344
Philippines	8,718
Poland	8,600
China	7,080
Taiwan	6,038
Britain	5,474
U.S.A.	5,317
Iran	5,133
TOP TEN	96,437
ALL SOURCES	186,044

* to 30 September
Reprinted by permission of
Employment and Immigration Canada.

Appendix 2
VISITOR VISA REQUIREMENTS AND VISA OFFICES

Country	Visa Office	Visitor Visa?
Afghanistan	Islamabad	Yes
Albania	Belgrade	Yes
Algeria	Rabat	Yes
Andorra	Madrid	No
Angola	Abidjan	Yes
Antigua and Barbuda	Bridgetown	No
Argentina	Buenos Aires	Yes
Aruba	Bogota	No
Australia	Sydney	No
Austria	Vienna	No
Azerbaijan	Moscow	Yes
Bahamas	Kingston	No
Baharain	Riyadh	Yes
Bangladesh	New Delhi	Yes
Barbados	Bridgetown	No
Belarus	Moscow	Yes
Belgium	Brussels	No
Belize	Kingston	Yes
Benin	Abidjan	Yes
Bermuda	New York	No
Bhutan	New Delhi	Yes
Bolivia	Lima	Yes
Bosnia-Hercegovina	Belgrade	Yes
Botswana	Pretoria	No
Brazil	Sao Paulo	Yes
British Virgin Islands	Bridgetown	No
Brunei	Nairobi	No
Bulgaria	Belgrade	Yes
Burkina-Faso	Abidjan	Yes
Burundi	Nairobi	Yes
Cameroun	Abidjan	Yes
Cape Verde	Abidjan	Yes
Cayman Islands	Kingston	No
Central African Republic	Abidjan	Yes
Chad	Abidjan	Yes

Country	Visa Office	Visitor Visa?
Chile	Santiago	Yes
China	(see note 1)	Yes
Colombia	Bogota	Yes
Commonwealth of Independent States	Moscow	Yes
Comoros	Nairobi	Yes
Congo	Abidjan	Yes
Costa Rica	San Jose	No
Croatia	Belgrade	Yes
Cuba	Mexico City	Yes
Cyprus	Tel Aviv	No
Czech Republic	Prague	Yes
Denmark	Copenhagen	No
Djibouti	Nairobi	Yes
Dominica	Bridgetown	No
Dominican Republic	Port-au-Prince	Yes
Ecuador	Bogota	Yes
Egypt	Cairo	Yes
El Salvador	Guatemala City	Yes
Equatorial Guinea	Abidjan	Yes
Estonia	Moscow	Yes
Ethiopia	Nairobi	Yes
Fiji	Sydney	Yes
Finland	Helsinki	No
France	Paris	No
French Guiana	Port-au-Prince	No
French Polynesia	Sydney	No
Gabon	Abidjan	Yes
Gambia	Abidjan	Yes
Germany	Bonn	No
Ghana	Abidjan	Yes
Gibraltar	Madrid	No
Great Britain	London	No
Greece	Athens	No
Greenland	Stockholm	No
Grenada	Bridgetown	No
Guatemala	Guatemala City	Yes

Country	Visa Office	Visitor Visa?
Guinea	Abidjan	Yes
Guinea-Bissau	Abidjan	Yes
Guyana	Port of Spain	Yes
Haiti	Port-au-Prince	Yes
Honduras	San Jose	Yes
Hong Kong	Hong Kong	No
Hungary	Budapest	Yes
Iceland	Stockholm	No
India	New Delhi	Yes
Indonesia	Singapore	Yes
Iran	Damascus	Yes
Iraq	Damascus	Yes
Ireland	Dublin	No
Israel	Tel Aviv	No
Italy	Rome	No
Ivory Coast	Abidjan	Yes
Jamaica	Kingston	Yes
Japan	Tokyo	No
Jordan	Damascus	Yes
Kampuchea	Bangkok	Yes
Kenya	Nairobi	Yes
Khazakstan	Moscow	Yes
Kiribati	Sydney	No
Korea (North)	Seoul	Yes
Korea (South)	Seoul	Yes
Kuwait	Damascus	Yes
Kyrgystan	Moscow	Yes
Laos	Bangkok	Yes
Latvia	Moscow	Yes
Lebanon	Damascus	Yes
Lesotho	Pretoria	Yes
Liberia	Abidjan	Yes
Libya	Rome	Yes
Liechtenstein	Berne	No
Lithuania	Moscow	Yes
Luxembourg	Brussels	No

Country	Visa Office	Visitor Visa?
Macao	Hong Kong	Yes
Malagasay	Nairobi	Yes
Malawi	Nairobi	Yes
Malaysia	Kuala Lumpur	No
Maldives	Colombo	Yes
Mali	Abidjan	Yes
Malta	Rome	No
Marshall Islands	Sydney	No
Mauritania	Abidjan	Yes
Mauritius	Nairobi	No
Mexico	Mexico City	No
Micronesia	Tokyo	No
Moldova	Moscow	Yes
Monaco	Paris	No
Mongolia	Moscow	Yes
Morocco	Rabat	Yes
Mozambique	Nairobi	Yes
Myanamar	Bangkok	Yes
Namibia	Pretoria	No
Nauru	Sydney	No
Nepal	New Delhi	Yes
Netherlands	The Hague	No
Netherlands Antilles	Bogota	No
New Zealand	Sydney	No
Nicaragua	San Jose	Yes
Niger	Abidjan	Yes
Nigeria	Abidjan	Yes
Norway	Stockholm	No
Oman	Riyadh	Yes
Pakistan	Islamabad	Yes
Panama	San Jose	Yes
Papua New Guinea	Sydney	No
Paraguay	Santiago	Yes
Peru	Lima	Yes
Philippines	Manila	Yes
Poland	Warsaw	Yes
Portugal	Lisbon	Yes

Country	Visa Office	Visitor Visa?
Qatar	Riyadh	Yes
Reunion	Nairobi	No
Romania	Bucharest	Yes
Russia	Moscow	Yes
Rwanda	Nairobi	Yes
St. Kitts–Nevis	Bridgetown	No
St. Lucia	Bridgetown	No
St. Pierre et Miquelon	Boston	No
St. Vincent and Grenadines	Bridgetown	No
San Marino	Rome	No
Sao Tome e Principe	Abidjan	Yes
Saudi Arabia	Riyadh	No
Senegal	Abidjan	Yes
Seychelles	Nairobi	Yes
Sierra Leone	Abidjan	Yes
Singapore	Singapore	No
Slovakia	Prague	Yes
Slovenia	Belgrade	Yes
Solomon Islands	Sydney	No
Somalia	Nairobi	Yes
South Africa	Pretoria	Yes
Spain	Madrid	No
Sri Lanka	Colombo	Yes
Sudan	Cairo	Yes
Suriname	Port of Spain	Yes
Swaziland	Pretoria	No
Sweden	Stockholm	No
Switzerland	Berne	No
Syria	Damascus	Yes
Taiwan	Hong Kong	Yes
Tajikstan	Moscow	Yes
Tanzania	Nairobi	Yes
Thailand	Bangkok	Yes
Togo	Abidjan	Yes
Tonga	Sydney	Yes
Trinidad and Tobago	Port of Spain	Yes
Tunisia	Rabat	Yes
Turkey	Ankara	Yes

Country	Visa Office	Visitor Visa?
Turkmenistan	Moscow	Yes
Turks and Caicos	Kingston	No
Tuvalu	Sydney	No
Uganda	Nairobi	Yes
Ukraine	Kiev	Yes
United Arab Emirates	Riyadh	Yes
United States of America	(see note 2)	No
Uruguay	Buenos Aires	Yes
Uzbekistan	Moscow	Yes
Vanuatu	Sydney	No
Vatican	Rome	No
Venezuela	Bogota	No
Vietnam	Bangkok	Yes
Western Samoa	Sydney	No
Yemen	Riyadh	Yes
Yugoslavia	Belgrade	Yes
Zaire	Abidjan	Yes
Zambia	Nairobi	Yes
Zimbabwe	Pretoria	No

NOTE 1:
CHINA – All provinces except Guanxi and Guangdong – Beijing; Guangxi and Guangdong – Hong Kong.

NOTE 2:
UNITED STATES OF AMERICA

State	Visa Office
Alabama	Atlanta
Alaska	Seattle
Arizona	Los Angeles
Arkansas	Dallas
California	Los Angeles
Colorado	Los Angeles
Connecticut	New York
Delaware	Washington
District of Columbia	Washington
Florida	Atlanta

Country	Visa Office
Georgia	Atlanta
Hawaii	Los Angeles
Idaho	Seattle
Illinois	Chicago
Indiana	(see note 3)
Iowa	Minneapolis
Kansas	Dallas
Kentucky	Detroit
Louisiana	Dallas
Maine	Boston
Maryland	Washington
Massachusetts	Boston
Michigan	Detroit
Minnesota	Minneapolis
Mississippi	Atlanta
Missouri	Chicago
Montana	Minneapolis
Nebraska	Minneapolis
Nevada	Los Angeles
New Hampshire	Boston
New Jersey	New York
New Mexico	Dallas
New York	(see note 4)
North Carolina	Atlanta
North Dakota	Minneapolis
Ohio	Detroit
Oklahoma	Dallas
Oregon	Seattle
Pacific Islands	Tokyo
Pennsylvania	(see note 5)
Puerto Rico	Atlanta
Rhode Island	Boston
South Carolina	Atlanta
South Dakota	Minneapolis
Tennessee	Atlanta
Texas	Dallas
Utah	Los Angeles
Vermont	Boston
Virginia	Washington

Country	Visa Office
Virgin Islands	Atlanta
Washington	Seattle
West Virginia	Washington
Wisconsin	Chicago
Wyoming	Los Angeles

NOTE 3:
INDIANA

County	Visa Office
Jasper, Lake, Laporte, Newton, Porter	Chicago
All others	Detroit

NOTE 4:
NEW YORK

Area	Visa Office
Southeast part	New York
West and North	Buffalo

NOTE 5:
PENNSYLVANIA

Area	Visa Office
Eastern part	Washington
Western part	Buffalo

Reprinted by permission of Employment and Immigration Canada.

Appendix 3
CANADIAN EMBASSIES

Location	Address	Telephone/ Facsimile
Argentina	TAGLE 2828 P.O. Box 1598, 1000 Correo Central Buenos Aires	(54-1) 805-3032 F = 806-1209
Australia	Level 5, Quay West 111 Harrington St. Sydney, N.S.W. 2000	(61-2) 364-3050 F = 364-3099
Austria	Dr. Karl Lueger, Ring 10, A-1010 Vienne	(43-222) 533-3691 F = 535-4473
Barbados	Bishops Court Hill P.O. Box 404 Bridgetown	(809) 429-3550 F = 429-3780
Belgium	2 Tervuren Ave. Bruxelles 1040	(32-2) 735-60-40 F = 735-3383
Brazil	Edificio Top Centre Av. Paulista 854, 5th Fl. Caixa Postal 22002 Sao Paulo	(55-11) 287-2122 F = 251-5057
Chile	Ahumeda 11, 10th fl. Casilla 771 Santiago	(56-2) 696-2256 F = 696-0738
China	10 San Li Tun Road Chao Yang District Beijing	(86-1) 532-3536 F = 532-1684
Colombia	Aparto Aereo 052978 Calle 76, No. 11-52 Bogota 2	(57-1) 217-5555 F = 235-6253
Costa Rica	Cronos Bldg, 6th Fl. Calle 3 y Ave. Central A.P. 10303, San Jose	(506) 23-04-46 F = 23-23-95

Location	Address	Telephone/ Facsimile
Czech Republic	Mickiewiczova 6 Prague 6	(42-2) 32-6941 F = 34-1596
Denmark	Kr. Bernikowsgade 1 1105 Copenhagen K	(33) 12 22 99 F = (45-33) 14-05-85
Egypt	P.O. Box 2646 Gargen City Cairo	(20-2) 354-3110 F = 355-7276
Finland	Pohjois Esplanadi 258 P.O. Box 779 00100 Helsinki 10	(358-0) 17-11-41 F = 60-10-60
France	35, avenue Montaigne 75008 Paris	(33-1) 47-23-01-01 F = 47-23-56-28
Germany	Europa-Centre 1000 Berlin 30	(011-49-30) 261-1161 F = 262-9206
Germany	Godesberger Allee 119 5300 Bonn 2	(49-228) 23-10-61 F = 37-65-25
Greece	4 Ioannou Gennadiou St. Athens 11521	(30-1) 7239-511 F = 724-7123
Guatemala	7 Avenida 11-59, Zona 9 P.O. Box 400 Guatemala, C.A.	(502-2) 32-14-11 F = 32-14-19
Haiti	Bank of Nova Scotia Bldg. 18 Delmas St. P.O. Box 826 Port-au-Prince	(509-1) 2-2358 F = 3-8720 F = 17-5801
Hong Kong	8 Connaught Place, 11-14 fls. 1 Exchange Square P.O. Box 11142 Hong Kong	(852) 5-8104321 F = 810-6736
Hungary	Badakeszi Ut 32 Budapest 1121	(36-1) 1767-312 F = 1767-689

Location	Address	Telephone/ Facsimile
India	P.O. Box 5207 New Delhi 110021	(91-11) 687-6500 F = 687-6579
Ireland	65 St. Stephen's Green Dublin 2	(353-1) 78-19-88 F = 78-12-85
Israel	220 Hayarkon St. P.O. Box 6410 Tel Aviv 63405	(972-3) 228122 F = 527-2333
Italy	Via Zara, 30 00198 Rome	(3906) 440-3028 F = 884-8752
Ivory Coast	23 Nogues Ave. Trade Centre B.P. 4104 Abidjan 01	(224) 32-20-09 F = (225) 32-77-28
Jamaica	Royal Bank Bldg. 30-36 Knutsford Blvd. P.O. Box 1500 Kingston 10	(1-809) 926-1500- 1/2/3/4/5 F = 926-1702
Japan	3-38 Akasaka 7-Chome Minato-Ku Tokyo 107	(81-3) 408-2101 F = 479-5320
Kenya	Comcraft House Hailé Selassie Ave. P.O. Box 30481 Nairobi	(251-2) 33-40-33 F = 33-40-90
Korea	Kolon Bldg., 10th Fl. 45 Mugyo-dong P.O. Box 6299 Seoul 100	(82-2) 753-2605 F = 755-0686
Kuwait	P.O. Box 25281 13113 Safat Kuwait City	(965) 251-1451 F = 256-4167

Location	Address	Telephone/ Facsimile
Malaysia	P.O. Box 10990 50732 Kuala Lumpur	(60-3) 261-2000 F = 261-3428
Mexico	Apartado Postal 105-05 11560 Mexico D.F.	(52-5) 254-3288 F = 545-3105
Morocco	P.O. Box 709 Rabat-Agdal	(212-7) 77-13-75 F = 77-28-87
Netherlands	Parkstraat 25 2514JD The Hague	(31-70) 361-4111 F = 356-2853
Pakistan	G.P.O. Box 1042 Islamabad	(92) 82-11-01 F = (92-51) 82-34-66
Peru	Federico Gerdes 130 (Antes Calle Libertad) Miraflores Lima	(51-14) 44-40-15 F = 44-43-47
Philippines	Commercial Centre P.O. Box 901 Makati, Rizal Manila, 3117	(63-2) 815-9536 F = 815-9595
Poland	Ulica Matejki 1/5 Warsaw 00-481	(48-22) 29-80-51 F = 29-64-57
Portugal	144/56 Ave. da Liberdade, 2nd Fl. 1200 Lisbon	(351-1) 347-63-62 F = 347-6466
Romania	36 Nicolae Iorga P.O. Box 2966, P.O. No. 22 Bucharest 71118	(40-0) 50-65-80
Russia	23 Starokonyushenny Pereulok Moscow	(7-095) 241-5070 F = 241-9155
Saudi Arabia	P.O. Box 94321 Riyadh 11693	(011-966-1) 488-2288 F = 488-1361

Location	Address	Telephone/ Facsimile
Singapore	Robinson Rd., P.O. Box 845 Singapore 9016	(65) 225-6363 F = 225-2450
Slovak Republic	Mickiewiczova 6 Prague 6	(42-2) 32-6941 F = 34-1596
South Africa	Nedbank Plaza, 4th Fl. P.O. Box 26006, Arcadia Pretoria 0007	(27-12) 324-3970 F = 323-1564
Spain	Edificio Goya Nunez de Balboa 35 Apartado 587 28001 Madrid	(34-1) 431-4300 F = 431-2367
Sri Lanka	P.O. Box 1006 6 Gregory's Road Cinnamon Gardens Colombo 7	(94-1) 69-58-41/42 F = 50-26-43
Sweden	P.O. Box 16129 S10323 Stockholm 16	(46-8) 23-79-20 F = 24-24-91
Switzerland	11 Belpstrasse P.O. Box 1261 3001 Berne	(41-31) 25-22-61 F = 44-73-15
Syria	Autostrade Mezzeh, Lot 12 P.O. Box 3394 Damascus	(963-11) 33-05-35 F = 33-05-35
Thailand	138 Silom Road P.O. Box 2090 Bangkok 10500	(66-2) 234-1561 F = 236-6463
Trinidad and Tobago	Colonial Bldg. 72-74 South Quay P.O. Box 565 Port of Spain	(809) 625-1941 Ext. 7 F = 624-4016

Location	Address	Telephone/ Facsimile
Turkey	Nenehatun Caddesi No. 75 Gaziosmanpasa Ankara	(90-4) 136-1275 F = 146-4437
Ukraine	2 Howtneva Hotel, Rm 808 Box 200 Kiev 252001	
United Kingdom	38 Grosvenor Square London W1X 0AA England	(44-71) 629-9492 F = 491-7861
Yugoslavia	Kneza Milosa 75 1100 Belgrade	(38-11) 644-666 F = 641-480

UNITED STATES

Atlanta	400 South Tower One CNN Center Atlanta, Georgia 30303	(404) 577-6810 F = 424-5046
Boston	3 Copley Place, Ste. 400 Boston, Massachusetts 02116	(617) 262-3760 F = 262-3415
Buffalo	1 Marine Midland Center, Buffalo, New York 14203-2884	(716) 852-1252 F = 852-4340
Chicago	Two Prudential Plaza 180 North Stetson Ave. Ste. 2400 Chicago, Illinois 60601	(312) 616-1860 F = (312) 616-1875
Dallas	St. Paul Tower, Ste. 1700 750 North St. Paul St. Dallas, Texas 75201	(214) 992-9818 F = 922-9815

Location	Address	Telephone/ Facsimile
Detroit	600 Renaissance Centre Detroit, Michigan 48243-1704	(313) 567-2340 F = 567-2164
Los Angeles	300 South Grand Ave. Los Angeles, California 90071	(213) 687-7432 F = 620-8827
Minneapolis	701-4th Avenue, S., #900 Minneapolis, Minnesota 55415	(612) 333-4641 F = 332-4061
New York	1251 Avenue of the Americas New York, New York 10020-1175	(212) 768-2400 F = 768-2440
Seattle	412 Plaza 600 Sixth & Stewart Seattle, Washington 98101-1286	(206) 443-1777 F = 443-1782
Washington	501 Pennsylvania Ave. N.W. Washington, District of Columbia 20001	(202) 682-1740 F = 682-7726

Reprinted by permission of Employment and Immigration Canada.

Appendix 4
COURTS OF CANADIAN CITIZENSHIP

Newfoundland

Box 75, 8th Floor
Atlantic Place
215 Water Street
St. John's, Nfld.
A1C 6C9
Tel: (709) 772-5566
Fax: (709) 772-2275

Prince Edward Island

Application Centre
Suite 316, Dominion Building
95 Queen Street
Charlottetown, P.E.I.
C1A 4A9
Tel: (902) 566-7188
Fax: not applicable

Nova Scotia

5281 Duke Street
Halifax, N.S.
B3J 3M1
Tel: (902) 426-2148
     (902) 426-6227
     (toll free in Nova Scotia)
Fax: (902) 426-5428

New Brunswick

Central Guaranty Trust Building
860 Main Street, Suite 503
Moncton, N.B.
E1C 1G2
Tel: (506) 851-7050
Fax: (506) 851-7079

Québec

Senior Citizenship Judge
Room 12A2, 25 Eddy Street
Hull, Qué.
K1A 1K5
Tel: (819) 953-2252
Fax: (819) 953-8386

Québec continued

Guy-Favreau Complex
200 René-Lévesque Boulevard West
10th Floor, West Tower
Montréal, Qué.
H2Z 1X4
Tel: (514) 283-6679
Fax: (514) 283-3449

5167 Jean-Talon Street East
Room 100
Montréal, Qué.
H1S 1K8
Tel: (514) 283-6817
Fax: (514) 283-3645

6420 Saint-Denis St.
Montréal, Qué.
H2S 2R7
Tel: (514) 283-6835
Fax: (514) 283-3646

Saint-Amable Complex
333 Saint-Amable St.
Suite 155
Québec City, Qué.
G1R 5G2
Tel: (418) 648-3831
Fax: (418) 648-5535

Ontario

150 Main Street West
Room 412
Hamilton, Ont.
L8P 1H8
Tel: (416) 572-2361
Fax: (416) 572-4345

106 Clarence Street,
Suite 210
Kingston, Ont.
K7L 1X3
Tel: (613) 545-8015
Fax: (613) 545-8187

Ontario continued

Government of Canada Building
Main Floor
451 Talbot Street
London, Ont.
N6A 5C9
Tel: (519) 645-4334
Fax: (519) 645-5566

77 City Centre Drive
Suite 151
Mississauga, Ont.
L5B 1M5
Tel: (416) 973-6424
Fax: (416) 277-6439

4580 Dufferin Street
Suite 300
North York, Ont.
M3H 5Y2
Tel: (416) 973-6424
Fax: (416) 665-4032

310 Simcoe St. South
2nd Floor
Oshawa, Ont.
L1H 4H7
Tel: (416) 723-1216
Fax: (416) 433-1082

150 Kent Street, 9th Floor
Ottawa, Ont.
K1A 0M5
Tel: (613) 992-4485
Fax: (613) 996-9255

Canada Centre Bldg.
200 Town Centre Court
Suite 217
Scarborough, Ont.
M1P 4X8
Tel: (416) 973-6424
Fax: (416) 973-5123

Ontario continued

Federal Building
19 Lisgar Street South, Room 326
Sudbury, Ont.
P3E 3L4
Tel: (705) 671-0621
Fax: (705) 671-0620

Federal Building
33 South Court Street, Room 234
Thunder Bay, Ont.
P7B 2W6
Tel: (807) 345-2316
Fax: (807) 345-9731

55 St. Clair Ave. East, Suite 216
Toronto, Ont.
M4T 1M2
Tel: (416) 973-6424
Fax: (416) 973-7540

Application Centre
1541 Bloor St. West
Toronto, Ont.
M6P 1A5
Tel: (416) 973-6424
Fax: (416) 537-4735

70 King Street North
Waterloo, Ont.
N2J 2X0
Tel: (519) 886-3120
Fax: (519) 886-8097

467 University Ave. West
Room 201
Windsor, Ont.
N9A 5R2
Inf: (519) 252-7852
Fax: (519) 252-7977

Manitoba	Canadian Grain Commission Bldg. 303 Main Street, Room 200 Winnipeg, Man. R3C 3G7 Tel: (204) 983-3792 Fax: (204) 983-5365
Saskatchewan	2101 Scarth Street Room 200 Regina, Sask. S4P 2H9 Tel: (306) 780-5535 Fax: (306) 780-6630
	Financial Building 230-22nd Street East Room 505 Saskatoon, Sask. S7K 0E9 Tel: (306) 975-4115 Fax: not applicable
Alberta	220-4th Avenue S.E. Room 254 Calgary, Alta. T2P 3C1 Tel: (403) 292-5539 Fax: (403) 292-5543
	9700 Jasper Avenue Suite 225 Edmonton, Alta. T5J 4C3 Tel: (403) 495-3355 Fax: (403) 495-4873
British Columbia	102-1433 St. Paul St. Kelowna, B.C. V1Y 2E4 Tel: (604) 861-3317 Fax: not applicable

British Columbia continued

Royal Bank Building
550 Victoria Street
Suite 400A
Prince George, B.C.
V2L 2K1
Tel: (604) 561-5303
Fax: not applicable

7093 King George Highway
Suite 240
Surrey, B.C.
V3W 5A2
Tel: (604) 775-7005
Fax: (604) 775-7013

Sinclair Centre
757 West Hastings St., Suite 200
Vancouver, B.C.
V6C 1A1
Tel: (604) 666-3971
Fax: (604) 666-6168

Customs House
816 Government St., Room 105
Victoria, B.C.
V8W 1W9
Tel: (604) 363-3464
Fax: (604) 363-3405

Yukon

4114 Fourth Avenue, Room 304
Whitehorse, Y.T.
Y1A 4N7
Tel: (403) 668-2721
Fax: not applicable

Northwest Territories

Scotia Centre
#4, 5102-50th Avenue, Room 202
Yellowknife, N.W.T.
X1A 3S8
Tel: (403) 920-8270
Fax: (403) 920-8399

Registrar of Canadian Citizenship

Multiculturalism and Citizenship
Canada
Ottawa, Ont.
KIA IK5
Tel: (819) 994-2869
Fax: (819) 953-8386

Reprinted by permission of Multiculturalism and Citizenship Canada.

Appendix 5
GOVERNORS GENERAL OF CANADA
SINCE CONFEDERATION

Name	Assumed Office
1. The Viscount Monck, GCMG	*1 July 1867*
2. Lord Lisgar, GCMG	*2 February 1869*
3. The Earl of Dufferin, KP, GCMG, KCB	*25 June 1872*
4. The Marquess of Lorne, KT, GCMG	*25 November 1878*
5. The Marquess of Lansdowne, GCMG	*23 October 1883*
6. Lord Stanley of Preston, GCB	*11 June 1888*
7. The Earl of Aberdeen, KT, GCMG	*18 September 1893*
8. The Earl of Minto, GCMG	*12 November 1898*
9. The Earl Grey, GCMG	*10 December 1904*
10. Field Marshal H.R.H. The Duke of Connaught, KG	*13 October 1911*
11. The Duke of Devonshire, KG, GCMG, GCVO	*11 November 1916*
12. Gen. The Lord Byng of Vimy, GCB, GCMG, MVO	*11 August 1921*
13. Viscount Willingdon of Ratton, GCSI, GCIE, GBE	*2 October 1926*
14. The Earl of Bessborough, GCMG	*4 April 1931*
15. Lord Tweedsmuir of Elsfield, GCMG, GCVO, CH	*2 November 1935*
16. Maj. Gen. The Earl of Athlone, KG, PC, GCB, GCMG, GCVO, DSO	*21 June 1940*
17. Field Marshal the Rt. Hon. Viscount Alexander of Tunis, KG, GCB, GCMG, CSI, DSO, MC, LLD, ADC	*2 April 1946*

Name	Assumed Office
18. The Rt. Hon. Vincent Massey, PC, CH	*28 February 1952*
19. Maj. Gen. The Rt. Hon. Georges Philias Vanier, PC, DSO, MC, CD	*15 September 1959*
20. The Rt. Hon. Daniel Roland Michener, PC, CC	*17 April 1967*
21. The Rt. Hon. Jules Léger, CC, CCM	*14 January 1974*
22. The Rt. Hon. Edward Richard Schreyer, PC, CC,CMM, CD	*22 January 1979*
23. The Rt. Hon. Jeanne Sauvé, PC, CC, CMM, CD	*14 May 1984*
24. The Rt. Hon. Ramon John Hnatyshyn, PC, CC, CMM, CD, QC	*29 January 1990*

Reprinted by permission of Multiculturalism and Citizenship Canada.

Appendix 6

CANADIAN PRIME MINISTERS SINCE 1867

1.	Rt. Hon. Sir John A. Macdonald	Liberal-Conservative	1 July 1867 to 5 November 1873
2.	Hon. Alexander Mackenzie*	Liberal	7 November 1873 to 8 October 1878
3.	Rt. Hon. Sir John A. Macdonald	Liberal-Conservative	17 October 1878 to 6 June 1891
4.	Hon. Sir John J.C. Abbott*	Liberal-Conservative	16 June 1891 to 24 November 1892
5.	Rt. Hon. Sir John S.D. Thompson	Liberal-Conservative	5 December 1892 to 12 December 1894
6.	Hon. Sir Mackenzie Bowell*	Conservative	21 December 1894 to 27 April 1896
7.	Rt. Hon. Sir Charles Tupper* (Baronet)	Conservative	1 May 1896 to 8 July 1896
8.	Rt. Hon. Sir Wilfrid Laurier	Liberal	11 July 1896 to 6 October 1911
9.	Rt. Hon. Sir Robert L. Borden	Conservative	10 October 1911 to 12 October 1917
10.	Rt. Hon. Sir Robert L. Borden	Conservative**	12 October 1917 to 10 July 1920
11.	Rt. Hon. Arthur Meighen	Conservative	10 July 1920 to 29 December 1921
12.	Rt. Hon. William Lyon Mackenzie King	Liberal	29 December 1921 to 28 June 1926
13.	Rt. Hon. Arthur Meighen	Conservative	29 June 1926 to 25 September 1926
14.	Rt. Hon. William Lyon Mackenzie King	Liberal	25 September 1926 to 7 August 1930

15.	Rt. Hon. Richard Bedford Bennett (became Viscount Bennett 1941)	Conservative	7 August 1930 to 23 October 1935
16.	Rt. Hon. William Lyon Mackenzie King	Liberal	23 October 1935 to 15 November 1948
17.	Rt. Hon. Louis Stephen St. Laurent	Liberal	15 November 1948 to 21 June 1957
18.	Rt. Hon. John G. Diefenbaker	Progressive Conservative	21 June 1957 to 22 April 1963
19.	Rt. Hon. Lester B. Pearson	Liberal	22 April 1963 to 20 April 1968
20.	Rt. Hon. Pierre Elliott Trudeau	Liberal	20 April 1968 to 4 June 1979
21.	Rt. Hon. Charles Joseph Clark	Progressive Conservative	4 June 1979 to 3 March 1980
22.	Rt. Hon. Pierre Elliott Trudeau	Liberal	3 March 1980 to 30 June 1984
23.	Rt. Hon. John Napier Turner	Liberal	30 June 1984 to 17 September 1984
24.	Rt. Hon. Martin Brian Mulroney	Progressive Conservative	17 September 1984 to present

* Prior to 1968, "Right Honourable" was accorded only to Prime Ministers who had been sworn into the Privy Council for the U.K. Prime Ministers Mackenzie, Abbott and Bowell were only members of the Canadian Privy Council and Prime Minister Tupper became a U.K. Privy Councillor after his term as Canada's Prime Minister.

** During his second period in office, Prime Minister Borden headed a coalition government.

Reprinted by permission of Multiculturalism and Citizenship Canada.

Appendix 7
CANADA'S INCOME SECURITY PROGRAMS

Canadian residents may qualify for one or both government pension plans. These are:

1. Old Age Security.
2. The Canada Pension Plan (for most of Canada); **Quebec Pension Plan** (in Quebec).

The Canada Pension Plan (CPP) is a contributory plan. Benefits are based on various factors related to contributions and working years in Canada. Benefits are normally paid at age 65, but those who retire early may collect the pension as early as age 60 — at a reduced rate. Others may choose to postpone their retirement and start collecting the pension as late as age 70 — and receive a much higher benefit.

The Canada Pension Plan pays a monthly retirement benefit plus a one-time death benefit and monthly benefits for the families of the deceased, for the severely disabled and for their families.

Unlike the old age pension, there is no minimum Canadian residence required to collect CPP benefits when living abroad. The plan has been in force since January 1, 1966.

The Old Age Security Pension, established January 1, 1952, is based solely on Canadian residence. In contrast to the CPP, no contributions are required. All who meet basic residence conditions are entitled to collect a full or partial pension at age 65.

Applicants must be Canadian citizens or permanent residents at the time of the application. Normally, applicants must have lived in Canada for ten years to collect the pension while living in Canada, and 20 years to collect the pension while living abroad.

Old Age Security benefits are payable monthly and indexed quarterly to reflect increases in cost of living. Benefits are paid under two formulas:

A full pension is payable to persons 65 and over who have lived in Canada for a total of 40 years after age 18. Otherwise, they receive a partial pension based on 1/40th for each year of Canadian residence after age 18.

However, others may qualify for a full pension if: they were 25 or over on July 1, 1977 and were living in Canada or held a valid immigrant visa by that date; or they had lived in Canada prior to that date, were 18 years of age and had resided in Canada for the ten years immediately prior to the approval of their application.

Those absent from Canada during the last decade also qualify for the full pension provided they were residents of Canada for the full year immediately prior to the approval of the application, and that their residence in Canada from age 18 to just prior to that last decade is at least three times the length of absence from Canada. Residence in Canada does not have to be in consecutiv years. An extended stay abroad of a temporary nature not exceeding one year is not deemed to be an absence for pension purposes.

Once a partial pension is approved additional residence will not increase it. However, pensioners with little or no income may qualify for the federal Guaranteed Income Supplement. Based on a sliding scale geared to income, the supplement can boost a tiny monthly pension by several hundred dollars.

Spouse's allowance

Those 60 and over, but under 65, and married to an Old Age Security pensioner may be eligible for a Spouse's Allowance geared to the couple's combined income and the claimant's residence in Canada. Benefits are also available to low-income widows or widowers of that age bracket who meet the normal residence requirements.

International agreements

Canada has agreements on pensions with several countries, which may allow people to qualify for benefits otherwise denied.

Such persons may use period of residence in a country with which Canada has a social security agreement to satisfy those requirements. The amount of the Old Age Security pension, however, is based solely on actual residence in Canada. Those who have made contributions to another country's social security system may also qualify for benefits under that country's programs.

Additional information on Canada's income security benefits and other federal government social programs may be obtained through Health and Welfare Canada officers in Canada or through Canadian consular operations abroad. At the time of going to press, the following countries had reciprocal agreements with Canada on pensions: Australia, Austria, Barbados, Belgium, Cyprus, Denmark, Dominica, Finland, France, Germany, Greece, Iceland, Ireland, Italy, Jamaica, Luxembourg, Malta, the Netherlands, Norway, Portugal, Saint Kitts and Nevis, Saint Lucia, Spain, Sweden and the United States.

Glossary

ADJUDICATOR: a person who chairs an immigration inquiry.

ADMISSION: entry to Canada as a visitor or immigrant.

APPLICATION: the formal filing of an application to be granted Canadian citizenship or an immigration status.

AUTHORIZATION: generally refers to permission to work or study in Canada.

CANADIAN CITIZEN: a person born in Canada, born abroad of a Canadian parent, or an immigrant who has been granted the citizenship of this country.

CEREMONY: the final stage of the citizenship process when the applicant attends the court ceremony to be granted Canadian citizenship.

CERTIFICATE OF CITIZENSHIP: a certificate identifying the bearer to be a citizen of Canada.

CHILD: the natural son or daughter of the sponsor; a child legally adopted before age 13.

CITIZENSHIP COURT: the place where a citizenship judge performs his duties under the Citizenship Act.

CITIZENSHIP INTERVIEW: refers to the second stage of the citizenship process when the applicant is interviewed briefly by a citizenship judge.

CITIZENSHIP JUDGE: a judge empowered with citizenship determination responsibilities and who presides at the citizenship granting ceremony.

CONVENTION REFUGEE: a person who fits the United Nations definition of refugee, namely, "a person who, by reason of a well-founded fear of persecution for reasons of race, religion, nationality, membership in a particular social group or political opinion, a) is outside the country of his nationality and is unable, or, by reason of such fear, is unwilling to avail himself of the protection of that country, or b) not having a country of nationality, is outside the country of his former habitual residence and is unable, or, by reason of such fear, is unwilling to return to that country."

DELAYED REGISTRATION: refers to a provision in the 1977 Citizenship Act by which those born abroad of a Canadian father or born out of wedlock to a Canadian mother, but were never registered as Canadians, may now claim Canadian citizenship.

DEPARTURE ORDER: a notice to leave Canada, normally issued to a visitor who has committed a minor infraction of immigration law. It requires the person to leave Canada but doesn't bar that person from immediately applying to re-enter Canada (of course, this is subject to approval by immigration authorities.)

DEPENDENT(S): the spouse of a prospective immigrant and/or dependent children.

DEPORTATION ORDER: an order for the removal of an illegal alien, visitor or permanent resident who has committed a serious violation of Canadian law. The order permanently bars that person from returning to Canada — unless he or she obtains ministerial consent.

DESIGNATED OCCUPATION: a job in an area of Canada deemed to be in short supply of workers in that field of work.

ENTREPRENEUR: a prospective immigrant who intends to buy a Canadian business or make a substantial investment in any commercial venture expected to create jobs for Canadians.

ENTRY: lawful admission of a visitor.

EXCLUSION ORDER: a removal order, more stringent than a departure notice, normally issued at port of entry to people having incomplete or unsatisfactory documents. An exclusion notice bars that person from seeking admission to Canada again for one year.

FAMILY CLASS: sponsorable close family members of a Canadian citizen or permanent resident.

FIANCÉ(E): the intended bride or groom of the Canadian sponsor.

GUARANTOR: Canadian citizen or permanent resident willing and able to provide necessary food, care and accommodation to relatives he or she wishes to sponsor to Canada.

IMMIGRANT: any foreigner intending to come to Canada permanently.

INVESTOR: a wealthy, prospective immigrant expected to contribute financially to the Canadian economy.

JOINT SPONSOR: a relative co-signing a sponsorship

when the primary sponsor doesn't have the necessary income for sponsorship purposes.

LANDED: a person lawfully admitted to Canada as a permanent resident.

MARRIAGE: union of two persons of the opposite sex. Does not include common-law relationships.

MINISTER: the person responsible for the implementation of citizenship and immigration law.

MINISTER'S PERMIT: authorization by the Minister of Immigration for a person to enter or remain in Canada when normal immigration regulations forbid it.

MINOR: a person who has not yet reached the age of 18.

PARENT: the father or mother of a child, whether or not the child is born in wedlock (may include an adoptive parent).

PERMANENT RESIDENT: an immigrant who is a legal resident but not a citizen of Canada.

PRIOR LEGISLATION: any act governing citizenship or immigration that was in force prior to the present act.

RECORD OF LANDING: the immigration document by which immigrants are allowed to legally settle in Canada.

REFUGEE CLAIMANT: a person seeking sanctuary in Canada.

REGISTRAR: the keeper of citizenship records.

REGISTRATION REQUIREMENT: a prior requirement that children born abroad of a Canadian father (or mother, if out of wedlock), be registered as a Canadian born outside Canada.

RESIDENCY: the fact of living in Canada on a permanent,

full-time basis, generally for a period of not less than six months.

SPONSOR: a Canadian resident who backs an application for an immigrant visa by a close family member. The sponsor is required to pledge financial responsibility for that person for a period of up to ten years.

STUDENT AUTHORIZATION: a visa to allow a foreigner to study in Canada.

UNDERTAKING: a commitment to provide basic assistance to those sponsored. A legally-binding pledge for a period of up to ten years.

VISITOR: a non-resident admitted to Canada for a temporary purpose.

WAR BRIDE: a foreign-born woman who automatically gained Canadian citizenship on January 1, 1947, because she had married a Canadian and settled in Canada prior to 1947.